THE PORTLAND WALKBOOK

THE PORTLAND

WALKBOOK

by PEGGY ROBINSON

Maps by Judith A. Farmer

VICTORIA HOUSE   Portland, Oregon

By the same author:
Profiles of Northwest Plants:
Food Uses, Medicinal Uses, and Legends

Thanks to Dan Robinson for facilitating these explorations.

Thanks to Hilary Raphael for reading the manuscript and offering many valuable suggestions.

Vicinity map by David Inkpen

CONTENTS

INTRODUCTION

The Portland area provides an amazing variety of terrain for walking—from mountaintops to flood plains. The walks described in this book wander along the shores of rivers, streams, and lakes; plod through marshes; penetrate forests; and climb extinct volcanoes. The settings for the walks range from tiny secluded pockets in highly urbanized settings, to undeveloped parcels of suburbia, to vast expanses of *de facto* wilderness. A few unusual gardens of special interest to nature lovers have been included, and there are two urban historical walks. Some of the locations described here are places to experience, rather than sites for strenuous hiking. In addition to their esthetic appeal, many are interesting historic sites.

Several hiking guides are already available for trips farther afield, but we found a need for a book which would provide information about the abundance of beautiful natural sites "in our own backyard."

There are many good reasons for walking and hiking near home:

- Minimizing auto transportation saves energy, money, and nerves, as well as helping to preserve air quality. Hikers tend to feel superior to those who indulge in motorized forms of outdoor recreation, ignoring the fact that they themselves often drive their cars more than 100 miles for a day's hike of 10 miles or less! Most of the walking locations in this book can be reached by local bus.

- Travel time is minimal. These walks near home can be taken on short notice—when the clouds suddenly lift at 2 o'clock in the afternoon, after work on a summer evening, even on a long lunch hour. They are good for days when the weather doesn't look promising enough to invest in a long drive to a trailhead.

- These sites are available year 'round, including the many months when mountain trails are snowed in.

- Many of these spots are actually less crowded than popular sites in the mountains and at the coast. (If you crave a beach experience, you may be surprised to learn that there are many miles of sandy beach right here in Portland!)

- In most cases these areas near Portland are less fragile (or more disturbed already) and can more easily withstand heavy use than alpine or coastal areas.

For all these reasons, you can usually have a more refreshing outdoor experience if you "stay home!"

Most of these trails are easy walking; any obvious difficulties that we observed have been mentioned. In view of our climate, it is not surprising to come across many muddy spots, so it's a good idea to wear boots or washable tennis shoes. (You can extend the range of your walk if you are willing to wade occasionally!)

Several of the walks included are true neighborhood gems, but not worth the trip if you live across town, and this has been noted in the descriptions. Therefore in deciding whether to take a particular walk, consider the total distance from where you live.

OTHER PLACES TO WALK

GOOD LOCATIONS EXCLUDED FROM THE BOOK

Two obvious walking locations are *not* described in this book because they are already well covered in other publications.

Columbia Gorge

The Columbia Gorge is a popular destination for Portland hikers. The U.S. Forest Service map, ''Forest Trails of the Columbia Gorge,'' provides detailed information on the more than 150 miles of trails. The map is available for a small charge at local Forest Service offices. *The Columbia Gorge, Short Trips and Trails* by Oral Bullard and Don Lowe (Touchstone Press, 1974) is an attractive book providing descriptions of trails on both sides of the Columbia River.

Downtown Walking Tours

There are several sources for walking tours of downtown Portland. One of the best is *Portland, A Historical Sketch and Guide* by Terence O'Donnell and Thomas Vaughn (Oregon Historical Society, 1976). This book includes three walking tours of downtown with historical and architectural information. If you prefer to take a guided tour, Portland Walking Tours, 223-1017, leads tours based on the information in the book.

The Portland Chamber of Commerce distributes a free ''Walking Tour Map with Guide to Points of Interest,'' compliments of Lipman's and The First National Bank.

BEYOND THE RANGE OF THE BOOK

The range of this book was rather arbitrarily set at a 30-mile radius from downtown Portland. Of course numerous good walks can be found just beyond this boundary, and we can't resist listing some of them:

- Willamette Valley National Wildlife Refuges: Baskett Slough, Ankeny, and William L. Finley
- Silver Falls State Park
- Bureau of Land Management trails in the Molalla River Drainage (brochure available from the BLM in Salem)
- Pacific University Arboretum along Wilson River Highway

- Old Wilson River Wagon Road and other Tillamook state Forest trails (brochure available from Oregon State Department of Forestry)
- Hiking trails in southeastern Clark County, Washington, on land belonging to the Washington Department of Natural Resources.

HOW TO FIND MORE WALKS

You will be glad to hear that all the good walks in the area are not included in this book! There are still many places for you to discover on your own.

Good General Locations

- **Beaches.** We have included our favorites, but there are many more miles of beach along the Columbia River waiting to be discovered by you.
- **Dikes.** These provide flat walking with wide views. They can be found along both shores of the Columbia and on Sauvie Island.
- **Country roads.** The faintest lines on your road map!
- **Cemeteries.** These open areas are often on hilltops which provide good vistas. Old tombstones (and the mosses and lichens growing on them) are often interesting.
- **Neighborhood history and architecture walks.** For example, contact the Neighborhood History Project, 2200 NE 24th, 282-4976, for walking tours of the Buckman or Sellwood neighborhoods.
- **Timber company lands in western Washington County.** These lands belong to various companies but are open for recreation unless posted otherwise. (Avoid during hunting season.) There are no designated hiking trails that we could locate, but there are many miles of old logging roads through forests of varying ages. The existence of this vast area compensates in part for the general dearth of large parks in Washington County.

Helpful Maps

Map study is a fascinating pursuit that can reveal many new places.

- A standard **Portland street map** available at service stations can be most useful.

- **County maps** published by the State Department of Transportation are the most detailed road maps available. They may be ordered for a nominal fee from:
  Department of Transportation
  Map Distribution Unit
  Room 17, Transportation Building
  Salem, OR 97310
  Send for an index and price list first, to make an intelligent choice.

- **U.S. Geological Survey Maps.** Scrutinize them for undeveloped areas with the type of topography that appeals to you (hills, creeks, etc.). These maps can be purchased in at least two Portland locations: J.K. Gill's downtown store and Captain's Nautical Supplies. If you don't want to buy them, the map room of the Multnomah County Library downtown has a complete collection for Oregon and Washington.

- **Willamette River Recreation Guide.** Map published by the Oregon State Highway Division and distributed free at Chambers of Commerce, etc.

- **Oregon Parks.** Map giving the location of most parks in the state plus information about their attractions and facilities. Also published by the State Highway Division and distributed free.

- **Portland Parks: Our City, an Oasis.** Map of Portland showing the location of all Portland city parks plus information about facilities. Published and distributed free by the Portland Park Bureau.

- **Clackamas County Parks.** A useful map and inventory of the many recreation areas in this large verdant county. Published by the county and distributed free at Chambers of Commerce, etc.

- **Kani O We [Outdoor Trails], an outdoor resource guide to Clark County.** This booklet prepared by the Campfire Girls of Clark County, Washington, provides comprehensive information about the diverse, extensive public lands in the county. Available free from Campfire Girls at 1310 E. Evergreen Blvd., Vancouver, WA 98661.

Useful maps available for specific areas are described under the individual walks.

OUTLOOK FOR NEW TRAILS

There are some exciting proposals for new trails. Many of these proposed trails are part of a grand design for a statewide, interconnected trail system to provide access from most major cities to outstanding scenic and recreational areas throughout Oregon. In 1971 the Oregon State Legislature passed the Recreation Trails System Act, authorizing the development of such a network. For more information about the project, contact the Coordinator of the Recreation Trails System in the State Parks and Recreation Branch in Salem. (It is encouraging that we have a full-time civil servant in charge of trail development!)

PORTLAND WATERFRONT. There have been many ambitious proposals for beautifying the downtown waterfront area, and hopefully some of them may come to pass. One proposal would provide closer access to the water by means of floating docks. Landscaping is being improved.

The Portland Planning Commission is currently considering and presenting for public discussion three different options for longer waterfront trails. One option would create three such trails:
- West shore trail from the Broadway Bridge south to the city limits
- East shore trail from the Burnside Bridge south to the city limits
- East shore trail from the Coliseum to Kelley Point Park

Implementation of these plans would necessitate the cooperation of a number of private landowners with holdings in significant locations. To get more information about future plans for the waterfront area and to express your views on the subject, contact the City Planning Office.

WEST HILLS TRAIL. This proposed 20-mile trail would link the entire west side of Portland by trail. Much of it would go through existing parks, starting with the Wildwood Trail in Forest Park and progressing as far as Tryon Creek State Park at the southern boundary of Portland. One important link in the trail would be the proposed *Marquam Nature Park*. A group of residents in the Marquam Hill area has been working to save from development this steep wooded canyon downhill from Council Crest.

Actually the West Hills Trail is part of an even larger dream of a trail from Portland across the Coast Range to the Oregon Coast!

COLUMBIA SLOUGH RECREATION PROJECT. A continuous park corridor is proposed, parallel to the Columbia River stretching from Kelley Point Park to the mouth of the Sandy River. The Portland

Park Bureau has commissioned a recreation plan for the area, and they are seeking citizen input.

LOOP MASTER PLAN. This ambitious plan is a belated attempt to realize a scheme first envisaged in 1903 for a ring of parks around Portland. The Olmsted Brothers, famous early city planners (most renowned for the design of Central Park in New York City) made the recommendation when they came to Portland to draw up plans for the 1905 Lewis & Clark Exposition. A 40-mile loop trail would link the Columbia Slough, Blue Lake, Fairview Creek, and Johnson Creek on the east side of the Willamette with the parks in the West Hills. The Portland Park Bureau and the City Council hope to spur a joint effort to finance and build the trail system by government agencies at county, state, and federal levels.

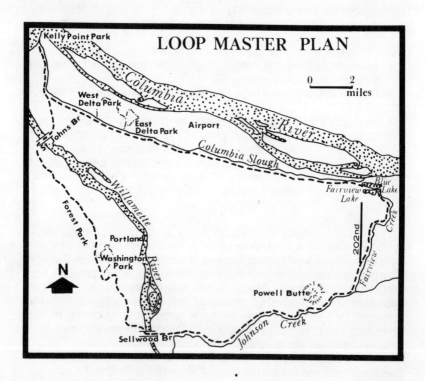

SANDY RIVER. A continuous trail along the Sandy River which would link up several existing sections of trail has been proposed.

COLUMBIA GORGE. There is also a proposal for a Columbia Gorge trail starting from the Columbia Slough in Portland, linking up with existing trails in state parks and national forest in the gorge, and continuing as far as The Dalles.

Expansion of the state park system will create other new hiking opportunities:

MOLALLA RIVER STATE PARK. The state has already acquired the land for this large natural park located near Canby at the junction of the Pudding, Molalla, and Willamette Rivers. This site is a wonderful wildlife habitat which includes a great blue heron nesting area and an extensive system of beaver ponds. So far, the park is completely undeveloped, and access on foot to most of it is impossible. The master development plan calls for some trails and bike paths, though the primary purpose of this park is "to preserve the scenic and wildlife values of the natural river flood plain."

BANKS TO VERNONIA LINEAR STATE PARK. The state has purchased this strip of land along an abandoned railroad right-of-way. Original plans called for a solid-surface trail appropriate for either bike riders or hikers. An entrance to the area is signed at Buxton, but so far it is not very pleasant walking because nothing has been done to modify the rough gravel of the railroad bed.

ST. MARY'S FOREST STATE PARK. The State Parks Branch is seeking funds for purchase of this natural marsh and woods in a prime urban location between Beaverton and Aloha. (See the walk description for St. Mary's Forest.)

A 1971 CRAG report, *The Urban Outdoors,* provides a useful survey of the remaining (in 1971!) undeveloped land which is suitable for parks and open space within our four-county urban area. After demonstrating the need for this land for open space, the report presented an optimistic ten-year schedule for public acquisition of these lands.

PROTECTION OF NATURAL AREAS

The walks described in this book provide easy opportunities for people who live in the Portland area to experience the natural world. Hopefully the more people who have this experience, the greater will be the commitment to preserve the opportunities. Of course, the reverse could be true, and this possibility haunts the author: Providing information about these sites could result in their destruction by crowds of irresponsible hikers.

We hope that our readers will disprove that scenario by showing the greatest respect for these natural areas that have fortuituously remained available to us. The various rules for responsible outdoor behavior can be summarized by the plea to ''let your presence remain undetected''—while you are there, as well as after you have left.

Beyond the immediate responsibility of refraining from destructive behavior while out walking are the larger responsibilities of participation in the land-use planning process to see that more lands are set aside, and vigilance to preserve those areas already in public ownership.

LAND USE PLANNING

It is vital that citizens who love the natural world, and want to see some segments of it remain, become involved in the often abstruse process of land use planning. This decade is a crucial era for the determination of future land use because all cities and counties in Oregon are presently working on comprehensive plans. These plans were mandated by the 1973 Oregon Legislature in establishing the Land Conservation and Development Commission. All plans must comply with 14 statewide goals. These include preservation of agricultural land, forest land, and open space and the protection of natural and scenic resources. Air and water quality are to be maintained. Recreation needs must be taken into account, with priority given to meeting the needs of residents of high-density population centers who have limited mobility and finances. These recreation activities must proceed with minimal use of energy and minimal environmental deterioration. Urban walks seem to meet these criteria very well!

Governmental planning agencies are required by law to vigorously seek citizen input into the planning process, and they often do make heroic efforts to simplify and explain the process to laypeople. Notices of hearings and informational meetings about land use issues are usually well-publicized in local papers. Copies of city and county land use plans can be obtained at planning offices or city halls.

If you live within the city of Portland, contact either the Planning Department or your local neighborhood association to find out where you can plug into the planning process for the comprehensive plan for Portland now being prepared.

It is also important to participate in planning at the county level, since there is still a good deal of undeveloped land outside the Portland city limits that could be reserved for parks or open space. County planning departments can tell you about the schedule for their comprehensive plans; or in Clackamas and Washington Counties, you can contact the Citizen Involvement Coordinators located in the county extension offices.

You can probably be most effective as a member of a neighborhood group in your locality or an environmental group such as the Oregon Environmental Council (see below).

Participation in the land use planning process may require a high degree of self-discipline for those of us who find the documents and meetings extremely tedious and would much prefer to spend our discretionary time out walking! But *it is important to be there* because, while professional planners have a mandate to weigh the views and needs of all segments of the community, those persons and groups favoring maximum development usually have more time and money, and hence more expertise, in promoting their views. Environmentalists are also at a psychological disadvantage because "action"—i.e. development—is more exciting than preserving the status quo.

Consider this striking statistic which emphasizes the crucial need for comprehensive land use planning in our area: The population of the Portland urban region *doubled* between 1940 and 1970, but the urbanized land area *quadrupled* during the same period. (*Atlas of Oregon*, p. 46.)

In addition to the governmental agencies working on land use planning, several private organizations fulfill a crucial role.

1000 Friends of Oregon is a nonprofit public interest organization founded in March 1975 to promote implementation and public understanding of Oregon's land use laws. Staff attorneys watchdog the activities of the LCDC, provide advice and assistance to local officials and citizens involved in planning, and give free legal representation in precedent-setting cases before the courts. They publish a *Newsletter* which provides current, detailed information on local planning activities, administrative rulings of LCDC, and decisions which are shaping Oregon's planning program.

The Nature Conservancy, a national organization with Northwest headquarters in Portland, identifies ecologically significant lands and then works to protect them. If public protection cannot be arranged, the Conservancy buys the endangered lands.

An important activity of the Nature Conservancy in Oregon is the Oregon Natural Heritage Program, which is surveying the entire state to locate all remaining areas of ecological significance. The purpose of the program is to identify sites containing unique or rare plant communities, rare or endangered wildlife, or significant habitats. This catalog of information, compiled on a county-by-county basis, is made available to local planning agencies to consider in drawing up their comprehensive plans.

The Oregon Environmental Council is a coalition of 80 conservation, planning and sportsmen's organizations plus thousands of individual citizens, committed to the preservation of a livable environment in Oregon. OEC lobbyists "confront political decisions at city, county, state, and federal levels of government." Their monthly newsletter, *Earthwatch Oregon,* is a good way to keep abreast of current environmental issues in Oregon.

Individual conservation organizations, such as local chapters of the Audubon Society and the Sierra Club, also play an important role in publicizing important environmental issues and exerting pressure on government.

The Sierra Club has produced a good general text, *The Grass Roots Primer: How to save your piece of the planet by the people who are already doing it* (James Robertson and John Lewallen, editors, Sierra Club Books, San Francisco, 1975). The section on "Steps to Power," pp. 201-254, gives particularly useful details about how to accomplish an environmental objective. One of the examples included in the book is the story of the successful citizen effort to establish Tryon Creek State Park.

PRESERVATION OF NATURAL VALUES IN EXISTING PARKS

While the land use planning process is vitally important because it can designate the use of appropriate lands for parks and open space, there is another aspect to the preservation of these lands once they have been set aside. The second crucial task of the nature lover is surveillance over those natural areas which are already supposed to be safely preserved as parks. Unfortunately the designation of "park" does not guarantee safety from encroachment for all time.

Parks departments are understaffed and underbudgeted, and with the best will in the world, they are often unable to take care of all the park land. Indeed, it is quite common for parks departments to be abolished during local government budget crises! When we called one local county parks department we were told, "Sorry, there is no parks department right now!"

There are constant pressures for public land to be "put to use." According to the current ethic, land which is not producing money is "wasted." Examples of this kind of thinking that come to mind are the recurrent controversy over allowing logging in Forest Park and the recent construction of a playing field and law school building by Lewis & Clark College on land that falls within the natural boundaries of Tryon Creek Park.

Internal park management decisions also have a crucial effect on the "natural" quality of a park. Decisions about what kinds of recreation will be promoted in a park determine how much land will be cleared for massive picnic installations, playing fields, campgrounds, roads, and parking areas. Often land seems to be cleared of natural vegetation for the sole purpose of "landscaping" —usually with native plants! The tranquillity of many beautiful parks is ruined and wildlife is discouraged by the noise of power mowers and chain saws used for "maintenance."

There are several ways to influence park management. The most obvious is to attend and testify at budget hearings. Another is to participate in citizens' advisory groups. The Portland Park Bureau has a Community Relations Coordinator working closely with neighborhood organizations. Hopefully the new volunteer programs in state and city parks will facilitate dialogue between citizens and park management. The volunteer program and public service employment programs are also providing hard-pressed parks departments with more manpower which could be used to enhance the natural values of these areas.

In conclusion, there are many treats in store for the walker who lives in the Portland area. We invite you to discover and enjoy these delightful places—and then appoint yourself their guardian!

NOTES ON THE HEADINGS

Walking Distance lets you know the maximum distance possible for walking. Remember, you don't have to go all the way!

Time to Spend is quite subjective and is included only to indicate a very rough idea of how long to allow. (Generally we like to spend almost as much time savoring the surroundings as actually walking.)

Setting. This is a capsule description of the kind of terrain covered by the walk, so you can choose a setting to fit your mood!

Distance from Downtown Portland was measured from the Morrison Bridge.

Driving Directions assume starting from downtown Portland.

Bus. We were happy to discover that most of the walking locations can be reached by bus, and we include this information to encourage walkers to leave their cars at home. Since bus routes are subject to change, call the bus company to confirm bus directions before setting out.

DOWNTOWN RIVERSIDE WALKS

Walking Distance	**West shore walk,** 1 mile one way
	East shore walk, ½ mile one way
Time to Spend	2-3 hours
Setting	Urban shoreline

Portland's waterfront promenades compare unfavorably with waterfront walks in other cities, but they are still worth exploring. Usually there are few people on these walkways, creating an eerie feeling of being in the middle of downtown but with lots of space around you. Access to the water line is rare because of the steep artificial embankments which have been constructed on both sides of the river to prevent flooding. Unfortunately it is not possible to make a loop trip which includes all or even most of both promenades. (A small loop of about 1 mile can be made using the Hawthorne and Morrison Bridges.)

Further implementation of the Willamette River Greenway may lead to a better system of paths here. (See "Outlook for New Trails" in the Introduction.)

WEST SHORE WALK

Park in the two-hour parking lot for the Public Small Boat Dock located at SW Clay St. and SW Harbor Dr., three blocks south of the Hawthorne Bridge. (If this lot is full, or you want to spend more than two hours, you can park in a six-hour lot on Front Ave. north of the Hawthorne Bridge.)

You can begin your walk by going out on the dock here for a closer look at the river or for a sunbath. The "classroom" boat of Portland Community College's Marine Engineering Technology Department is moored here. This dock is the only spot where you can get down off the embankment close to the water.

From the dock, walk north across a field to the promenade, which continues along the river past the Morrison Bridge and the Burnside Bridge, as far as the Steel Bridge.

At SW Oak St. you will come upon the mast of the battleship *Oregon,* a venerable ship which saw service in three major wars: the Spanish-American War, World War I, and World War II.

At the Burnside Bridge, you can detour for a visit to the Saturday Market spread out under the bridge across Front Avenue.

The harbor all along here used to be the scene of picturesque waterfront life: Steamships, sailing vessels, and riverboats landed here, and there were bustling stores, markets, banks, and saloons along the shore. In the 1930s the docks and waterfront buildings of early Portland were cleared away to be replaced by this sterile esplanade. The closure of Harbor Drive a couple of years ago was the first step in an ambitious plan to create a beautiful urban waterfront park for Portland. So far the widened "park" area is mostly mud and dead grass, but the potential exists for a very attractive park. There are nice vistas of the river from along the promenade, and sometimes you can go aboard one of the foreign naval vessels which anchor here.

EAST SHORE WALK

Walk or drive across the Hawthorne Bridge.

Driving: Take the Water Ave. turnoff from the bridge; go one block N along Water Ave.; turn L onto SE Madison St.; and drive to the parking area at the fireboat station at the end of the street.

Walking: Cross the Hawthorne Bridge on the *north* side; take the stairs going down to Water Ave. and SE Madison St.; turn R onto SE Madison; and go back to the right to the fireboat station.

In contrast to the west shore walkway, the shorter east shore walkway is attractively landscaped. In addition to river views, it offers interesting vistas of the downtown buildings across the river. This path parallels I-5 so is quite noisy. There is one place along here where you can walk down over rocks to a ledge close to the water level. The walkway ends abruptly before the Burnside Bridge.

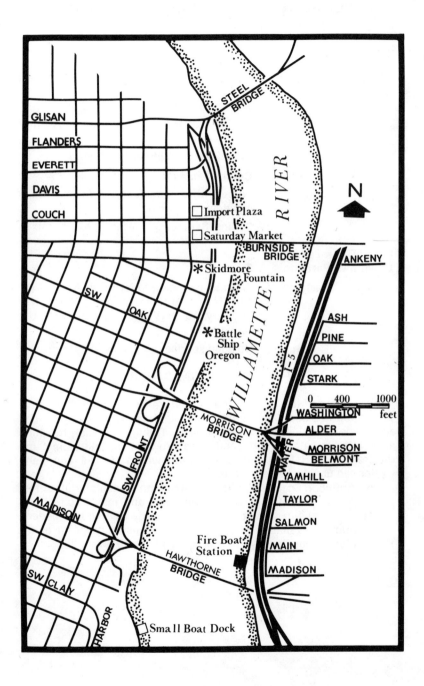

GLISAN
FLANDERS
EVERETT
DAVIS
COUCH

STEEL BRIDGE

RIVER

N

☐ Import Plaza
☐ Saturday Market

BURNSIDE BRIDGE

ANKENY

* Skidmore Fountain

SW

OAK

WILLAMETTE

* Battle Ship Oregon

I-5

ASH
PINE
OAK
STARK

0   400   1000
WASHINGTON   feet

ALDER

MORRISON BRIDGE

WATER

MORRISON
BELMONT

SW FRONT

YAMHILL
TAYLOR
SALMON

MADISON

MAIN

Fire Boat Station

MADISON

SW CLAY

HAWTHORNE BRIDGE

HARBOR

☐ Small Boat Dock

AUDUBON SOCIETY SANCTUARIES

These two sanctuaries are close together and can easily be explored in the same day.

Walking Distance   **Pittock Bird Sanctuary:** Several short trails to choose from; each is .6 miles or less, adding up to a total of 2 miles of trails.

Collins Sanctuary: 1-mile loop plus other short trails

Time to Spend   **Pittock Bird Sanctuary:** 1½ hours

Collins Sanctuary: 1 hour

Setting   **Pittock Bird Sanctuary:** Woods, creek meadow, wildlife pond

Collins Sanctuary: Second-growth mixed conifer forest

Distance from Downtown Portland   3½ miles

Driving Directions   W on W Burnside to NW 17th Ave.; R (N) on NW 17th to NW Lovejoy; L (W) on NW Lovejoy to NW Cornell Rd. to the sanctuaries.

Bus   No good service.

PITTOCK BIRD SANCTUARY

The setting of this 30-acre tract is naturalistic, though the native vegetation has been augmented with plantings to provide the food and cover attractive to a variety of birds. Though artificial, the pond area with its cattails and pond lilies provides an interesting and different habitat from the surrounding woods. Ducks and pond turtles can usually be seen here.

The Audubon Society clubhouse here contains exhibits of stuffed birds, nests, and eggs as well as butterfly and insect collections. From the glassed-in deck you can observe birds visiting the feeders. Information is available here about the extensive program of the Portland Audubon Society, of interest to all nature lovers.

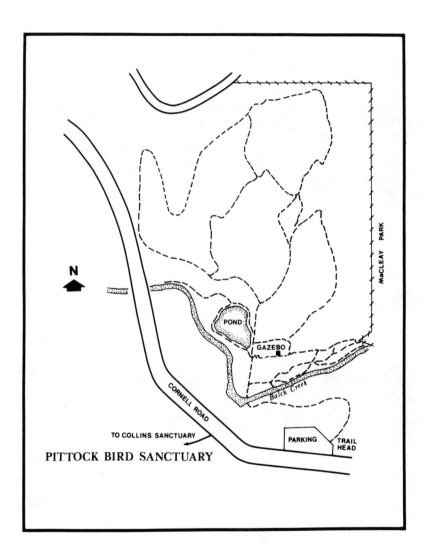

N

MaCLEAY PARK

POND

GAZEBO

Balch Creek

CORNELL ROAD

TO COLLINS SANCTUARY

PITTOCK BIRD SANCTUARY

PARKING

TRAIL HEAD

COLLINS SANCTUARY

This newly acquired area consists of 86 acres 100 yards up Cornell Rd. and across the street from the Pittock Sanctuary. The Collins Family Foundation donated the land to the Oregon Parks Foundation, which has leased it to the Audubon Society for $5 per year. Youth Conservation Corps workers built the foot bridge and refurbished the loop trail during the summer of 1977.

The Collins Sanctuary has had a checkered past. Homesteaded in the 19th century, logged in the 1940s, and used for racing by the Rose City Motorcycle Club in the 50s, it is now finally being allowed to return to a natural state, primarily because the ground is too unstable to be used for housing. (As you walk the trail look for curved tree trunks, indicating the trees' efforts to compensate for earth slippage.)

The Audubon Society has organized a Collins Sanctuary Study Group, which is studying the natural history of the area (and of Forest Park) and reporting on it in the *Warbler,* the Audubon Society newsletter.

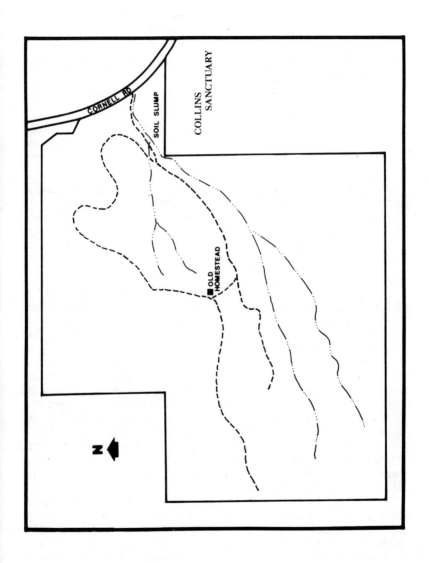

CORNELL RD

SOIL SLUMP

COLLINS SANCTUARY

OLD HOMESTEAD

N

FOREST PARK

Walking Distance	1-30 miles
Time to Spend	1 hour to 1 day
Setting	Varied second-growth forest. Steep canyons with occasional benches, but some trails along ridges are not steep.
Distance from Downtown Portland	3 or more miles depending on entrance used.
Driving Directions	Vary, depending on entrance used (see map).
Bus	#53, 23rd Ave. The end of the line at NW Thurman St. is near the bottom of Macleay Park and the beginning of Leif Erickson Drive.

Forest Park consists of more than 6000 acres of wilderness along a ridge separating the Tualatin Valley from the Willamette River. Though it is certainly the preeminent location for hiking in Portland, the park is presently underused. On a sunny summer weekend you may not find solitude in the mountains or at the beach, but you can find it here in Portland's backyard.

HISTORY AND MANAGEMENT

This magnificent park exists today by default—because other uses of the land never proved to be profitable. In the early part of the century, real estate developers had grandiose plans for subdivisions in the area, and it was during this period that Leif Erikson Drive was built. Subdivisions were platted along imaginary side roads, but were never developed because it proved too expensive to provide utilities across the rugged terrain. The cost of building Leif Erikson Drive also turned out to be excessive, and the property fronting it was assessed to pay for the road. Most of these assessments went unpaid, and this land reverted to city ownership.

Since much of the land was too steep and covered with soil too shallow for farming, after it was logged off, no one wanted it. This resulted in forfeiture of an additional large amount of land to Multnomah County for delinquent taxes.

Thus when the park was formed in 1947, 3000 acres, most of it contiguous, was already in public ownership (some in existing parks, such as Macleay Park). Since that time an additional 1200 acres have been acquired, leaving about 1900 acres of private land within the proposed park boundaries of Skyline Blvd., St. Helen's Rd., Cornell Rd., and Newberry Rd. (see map).

The city is trying to purchase these private parcels, and as one means to acquire the necessary funds, an agreement was concluded with the Rivergate Rock Company on St. Helen's Rd. permitting quarrying in Forest Park in return for royalties for the rock extracted. The royalty money is earmarked for land acquisition within the park boundaries. (An additional stipulation of the agreement is that the rock company is to reforest the area when quarrying is finished.)

Many city planners, from the Olmsted brothers in 1903 to Robert Moses in 1943, had recommended this area for a municipal forest park. The impetus to finally create the park came from a report issued by the City Club in 1944, containing a detailed plan which was adopted by the City Council in 1947. In the meantime, the Committee of 50, the influential advisory board which recommends policy for the park, was being organized. It was composed of forty representatives from civic, educational, and recreation organizations and businesses (including timber companies) plus ten members at large (including the five members of the City Club committee responsible for the report). The Committee of 50 still meets periodically, and in July 1976 issued its latest management plan for the park. This plan was adopted by the City Council as revised in November 1976.

There has been a great deal of controversy over how the park should be managed. The City Club report listed as one of the objectives of Forest Park "to grow timber which will in time yield an income and provide a demonstration forest." In 1950 the U.S. Forest Service was commissioned to prepare a Management Plan which recommended logging as well as the construction of ten campgrounds. Because of inertia and lack of continuity in administration, these plans were never carried out. In the 30 years since its creation, the park has been pretty well left alone and has become a *de facto* wilderness. The current conflict is between proponents of a "managed forest" and advocates of wilderness (which is valued more now than it was when the park was created).

In their 1976 *Management Plan for Forest Park,* the Committee of 50 recommended and the City Council approved the concept of a managed municipal forest. Management techniques would be designed to produce trees of optimum size and health and would include selective logging to remove dead trees, thin young stands, and provide scenic vistas as well as to control insects and disease. This approach would also include management of wildlife habitat; that is, changing of the forest by man to produce optimum conditions for attracting wildlife.

Other Portlanders vigorously oppose this concept and favor continuing the policy of benign neglect to let the park revert to primeval forest. They fear that foresters with their zeal for "improvement" will destroy the unique wilderness quality of the park. At the back of their minds looms the specter of large-scale logging (which probably would not be acceptable to the public today).

These issues aside, exciting plans are afoot for education programs in Forest Park. The Park Bureau has long-range plans for a visitor center and interpretive program in the park, and the

Portland Audubon Society is organizing a group to study the natural history of Forest Park.

For more information on the history and management of Forest Park consult the following sources (available in the Multnomah County Library):

Forest Park Committee of 50, *A Management Plan for Forest Park*, July 2, 1976.

Munger, Thornton T., *History of Portland's Forest Park*, 1960.

"Proposed Municipal Forest Park," *City Club Bulletin*, August 31, 1945.

VEGETATION

Because of its convenient location near early settlements and the Willamette River, the area was almost completely logged in the early days. At first the wood was used for domestic firewood and fuel for steamboats. Later it fed the many sawmills which were built along the river. The last logging took place in 1951. Hikers will come across huge old stumps with their springboard notches and traces of the old skid roads, which provide mute evidence of the logging of 100 years ago.

The major impact on the original vegetation has been fire—which has swept over the area many times. Fires were often caused by uncontrolled slash burning after logging. The last major fire (started from an abandoned campfire) burned uncontrolled for three days in September 1951, extending over 1200 acres of the park. After this devastation, new measures were taken for fire protection. These included constructing 12 miles of fire lanes down the main ridges, building water storage facilities, training Portland firemen in techniques for fighting forest fires, and setting up three lookout towers on the east side of the Willamette. (The lookouts were replaced by airborne fire patrols in 1969 when the city's smog became too thick for smoke to be identifiable from the towers.)

The effects of logging and fire account for the varied condition of the vegetation in the park. Miraculously, some old-growth Douglas fir can still be found. Much of the vegetation has regenerated to second-growth Douglas fir woodland. Other areas represent earlier successional stages, dominated by big-leaf maple or alder, and some areas are still brushy.

WILDLIFE

There is quite a variety of wildlife in the park, including deer, coyotes, bobcats, and a beaver colony, in addition to the common small mammals. Occasionally bear and elk wander into the area from the Coast Range. Many birds can be spotted, including grouse, quail, mourning doves, band-tailed pigeons, and pileated woodpeckers.

TRAILS

Printed Materials Useful in Planning Hikes in Forest Park

The items listed below are available from either the Park Bureau office downtown at SW 4th and Main or the Arboretum / Forest Park office on SW Fairview Blvd.

- Large map
- "Forest Park, A Self-guided Tour." Brochure containing a 6-mile driving or walking tour of Leif Erikson Drive (the road that bisects the park).
- "Portland's Forest Park Nature Trail." Teachers' guide to the Nature Trail prepared by the Oregon Outdoor Education Council.
- "The Kwonesum Nature Trail." Imaginative trail guide exemplifying the most modern concepts in environmental education, stressing sensory awareness and general ecological relationships rather than information.
- Wildwood Trail map and descriptive brochure; also available from the Western Forestry Center.

Another useful reference is

- *Guide to Trails and Roads of Forest Park,* Vol. I by Bill Keil. Out of print but available at the Multnomah County Library and branches. This handy little book is a detailed trail guide for the south half of Forest Park written by a man who was park forester during the 1950s.

General Trail System

Two major thoroughfares bisect the park from north to south: Leif Erickson Drive (unpaved and sometimes not passable by car) and the Wildwood Trail. Many short trails connect the two with each other and the Wildwood Trail with other access roads on the western boundary of the park. There is also a system of fire lanes running east-west which can be used for hiking. However, many of the firelanes are very precipitous and difficult to walk in wet weather when they are very muddy and slippery. Using the map, it is easy to plan your own loop trips.

The park is so large that most of the trails are never crowded.

Wildwood Trail

A hike along the entire Wildwood Trail will take you 16¾ miles along the ridgeline of the Tualatin Mountains from the Western Forestry Center through the Arboretum and Washington Park, past the Pittock Mansion, and on through Forest Park up to NW Salzman Rd. Eventually this trail will extend the entire length of Forest Park (nearly 30 miles).

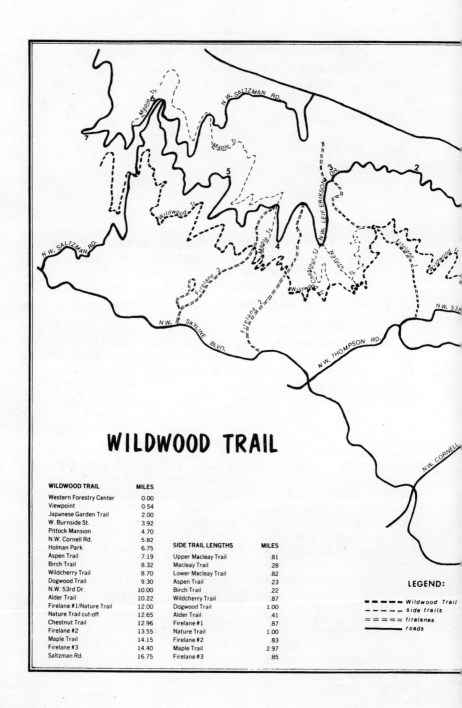

WILDWOOD TRAIL

WILDWOOD TRAIL	MILES
Western Forestry Center	0.00
Viewpoint	0.54
Japanese Garden Trail	2.00
W. Burnside St.	3.92
Pittock Mansion	4.70
N.W. Cornell Rd.	5.82
Holman Park	6.75
Aspen Trail	7.19
Birch Trail	8.32
Wildcherry Trail	8.70
Dogwood Trail	9.30
N.W. 53rd Dr.	10.00
Alder Trail	10.22
Firelane #1/Nature Trail	12.00
Nature Trail cut-off	12.65
Chestnut Trail	12.96
Firelane #2	13.55
Maple Trail	14.15
Firelane #3	14.40
Saltzman Rd.	16.75

SIDE TRAIL LENGTHS	MILES
Upper Macleay Trail	.81
Macleay Trail	.28
Lower Macleay Trail	.82
Aspen Trail	.23
Birch Trail	.22
Wildcherry Trail	.87
Dogwood Trail	1.00
Alder Trail	.41
Firelane #1	.87
Nature Trail	1.00
Firelane #2	.83
Maple Trail	2.97
Firelane #3	.85

LEGEND:

- ▄▄▄ Wildwood Trail
- ---- side trails
- ===== firelanes
- ——— roads

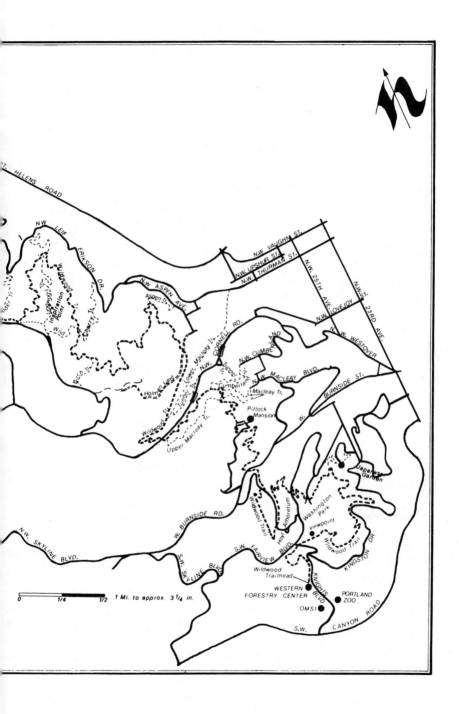

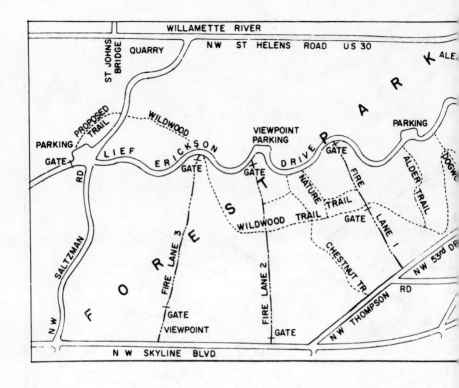

CUMBERLAND TRAIL
                               Miles

Cumberland Trail 0.0
Macleay Trail 0.4

TUNNEL TRAIL

Lower Macleay 0.0
Cornell Rd. 0.2
Cumberland Trail 0.5

LOWER MACLEAY TRAIL

Wildwood Trail 0.0
Tunnel Trail 0.1
Park Headquarters 0.6

BIRCH TRAIL

53rd Drive 0.0
Wildwood Trail 0.2

WILD CHERRY TRAIL

N.W. 53rd Dr. 0.0
Wildwood Trail 0.3
Leif Erickson Dr. 0.7
N.W. Alexandra . . . . : . . 0.9

DOGWOOD TRAIL

N.W. 53rd Dr. 0.0
Wildwood Trail 0.5
Leif Erickson Dr. 0.9

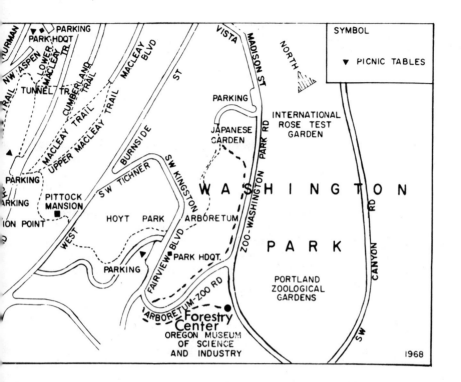

ALDER TRAIL

Wildwood Trail................. 0.0
Leif Erickson Dr. 0.0

CHESTNUT TRAIL

N.W. Thompson Rd. 0.0
Wildwood Trail................. 0.6
No Name Trail 0.9
Leif Erickson Dr. 1.1

WILDWOOD TRAIL

Western Forestry Center to
W. Burnside St. 3.92
W. Burnside to Pittock
Mansion 0.78
Pittock Mansion to Aspen Trail .. 2.49
Aspen Trail to Alder Trail 3.03
Alder Trail to Firelane No. 1 ..... 1.88
Firelane No. 1 to Maple Trail 2.15
Maple Trail to Salzman Rd. 2.60

The Wildwood Trail has been designated a National Recreation Trail by the Bureau of Outdoor Recreation, U.S. Department of the Interior.

Balch Canyon-Macleay Park

Approximately 1¼ miles one way. This walk through Balch Canyon is the prettiest in the park. It is also fairly well-known so may be crowded. The walk follows the Lower Macleay Trail from NW 29th Ave. and Upshur St. to its junction with the Wildwood Trail, then continues on the Wildwood Trail to emerge at Macleay Park on NW Cornell Rd. (Macleay Park was a city park in existence before Forest Park, which now encompasses it.)

Balch Creek is the largest stream in Forest Park. The creek bed is quite rocky, with numerous small cascades. This is an especially nice place to take children on a hot summer day. The creek is wonderful for wading and splashing and nowhere deep enough to be dangerous. Partway up the trail are the remains of an old stone building, perfect for children's fantasies. This canyon is also especially beautiful on the rare occasions when it snows in Portland.

Nature Trail

The Nature Trail provides several short convenient hiking loops (see map of nature trail area). The large loop is about 2¼ miles; each shorter loop is about 1¼ miles. The trail is used by local school systems, and a teachers' guide with information about the various numbered stations is available from the Park Bureau. (No information is available at the site.) A shelter, picnic tables, and restrooms are located near stop 20. Two road approaches are possible to the Nature Trail: via NW Cornell Rd. or NW Thompson Rd. to NW 53rd Dr. to Fire Lane 1, or via NW Thurman St. to Leif Erickson Dr. 3½ miles to Nature Trail (see maps).

Kwonesum Nature Trail

Not to be confused with the older Nature Trail mentioned above, the Kwonesum Nature Trail is a new trail set up in the north end of the park by students from the Environmental Education Center at Portland State University. This trail was sponsored by the Portland Metropolitan Environmental Education Committee. To get there, drive north on Skyline Blvd. to the junction with Newton Street. Drive down Newton about ¼ mile to a grassy area. Park there and follow signs for the trail. This is a pleasant loop of ¾ mile. It doesn't have special meaning for the visitor without the trail guide available from the Park Bureau (not available at the site).

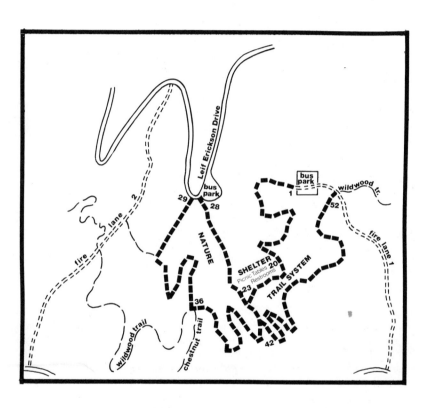

FORESTRY CENTER NATURE TRAIL

Walking Distance	⅓ mile
Time to Spend	½ hour
Setting	Wooded canyon
Driving Distance	2 miles
Distance from Downtown Portland	2 miles
Driving Directions	W on Highway 26 to OMSI exit.
Bus	#62, Zoo/OMSI

This trail provides a short walk in natural surroundings which can provide a pleasant change of pace when visiting one of the educational institutions in the area. The trail begins across the parking lot from the Western Forestry Center next to Tera I, the solar house.

There are no markers along the trail, but an attractive self-guiding brochure emphasizing broad ecological concepts is available from the education department at the Forestry Center.

HOYT ARBORETUM

Walking Distance	**Redwood Tour Trail:** 1 mile **Oak Tour Trail:** 1 mile **Joggers' Loop:** 3 miles **Wildwood Trail:** 3½ miles 8 miles of trail altogether in the Arboretum, including part of the Wildwood Trail (see Forest Park).
Time to Spend	½ day or more
Setting	Conifers and broad-leaved trees from all over the world planted among a native stand of Douglas fir, hemlock, and western red cedar. Rolling hills. Viewpoint of the city and mountains.
Distance from Downtown Portland	3 miles
Driving Directions	W on SW Canyon Rd. to Zoo/OMSI/Forestry Center exit. Continue on Knights Blvd. past OMSI and the Forestry Center up the hill to the junction with Fairview Blvd. Turn right onto Fairview, about 1000 feet to the parking lot and Visitor Center.
Bus	#62, Zoo-OMSI, is the closest. #76, Arlington, goes to the nearby Japanese Garden on weekdays.

VEGETATION

The Hoyt Arboretum is a scientific tree garden, containing more than 600 kinds of trees. The Arboretum's goal is to simulate nature in all the plantings, so most of the native trees, shrubs, ferns, and wildflowers have been carefully preserved and the specimen trees planted among them..This makes the Arboretum a good locale for either leisurely hiking or serious study of the plants. Wildflowers and many common birds can be found here in abundance.

Climatic conditions are obviously ideal here in Western Oregon for the growth of conifers, and our Arboretum contains the largest collection of distinct species of gymnosperms in the country. Some of the more unusual ones are the Brewer's weeping spruce, Cunninghamia, bristlecone pine, and dawn redwood (*Metasequoia glyptostroboides*). Fossil remains of the dawn redwood indicate that it grew in Oregon until the last Ice Age. Reintroduced from China in the 1940s, it flourishes here again. One of the dawn redwoods in the Arboretum produced the first cones in the Western Hemisphere in 50 million years.

Interesting broad-leaved trees include osage orange, loquat, Persian silk tree, and sassafras. Much of the planting stock comes from tree seeds sent from botanic gardens around the world. Distinct species of trees are planted rather than nursery varieties, so most planted trees appear as they do in their native countries.

A 10-acre plot of second-growth Douglas fir about 60 years old has been set aside as a primitive area on the south slope of the Arboretum along W. Burnside St. Future plans call for the establishment of a 50-acre area which will contain all trees native to the Northwest and another area with all the state trees of the United States which will tolerate our climate.

An "Arboretum Inventory" keyed to the Arboretum map can be consulted in the Arboretum office to locate any individual tree specimen. This is a good resource for botany and horticulture students.

HISTORY

The idea for a municipal arboretum was first proposed during Forestry Week in 1928 by a committee of tree lovers headed by Thornton T. Munger (later also to become the founding father of Forest Park). A parcel of 120 acres obtained from Multnomah County on the site of the former county poor farm has been gradually expanded to more than 200 acres. Much of the preliminary work of brush clearing, snag and stump removal, trail building, and leveling of picnic and nursery areas was accomplished by WPA labor during the Depression. The first plantings occurred in 1931, making the Hoyt Arboretum a "youngster" among the world's arboreta. It is remarkable what has been accomplished here in a short time by devoted curators, despite the fact that the Arboretum has always been understaffed and underbudgeted.

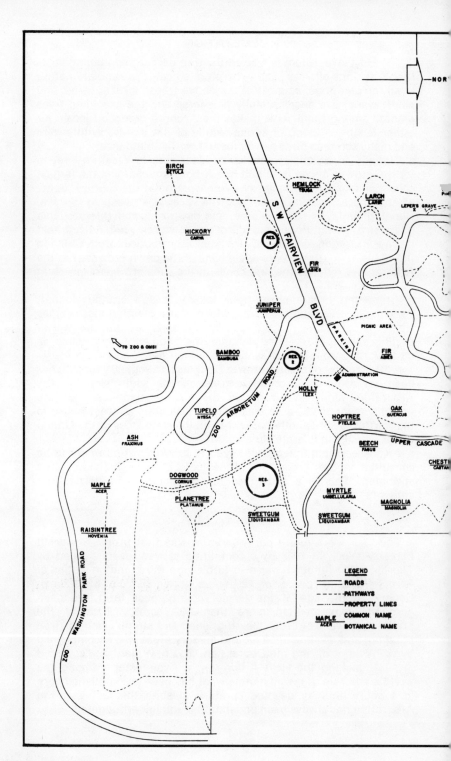

NOR[TH]

BIRCH
BETULA

HEMLOCK
TSUGA

LARCH
LARIX

LEPER'S GRAVE

HICKORY
CARYA

RES.
1

S W FAIRVIEW BLVD

FIR
ABIES

JUNIPER
JUNIPERUS

PICNIC AREA

TO ZOO & OMSI

BAMBOO
BAMBUSA

RES.
2

FIR
ABIES

ADMINISTRATION

HOLLY
ILEX

OAK
QUERCUS

TUPELO
NYSSA

ZOO - ARBORETUM ROAD

HOPTREE
PTELEA

ASH
FRAXINUS

BEECH
FAGUS

UPPER CASCADE

CHESTN[UT]
CASTAN[EA]

DOGWOOD
CORNUS

RES.
3

MAPLE
ACER

PLANETREE
PLATANUS

SWEETGUM
LIQUIDAMBAR

SWEETGUM
LIQUIDAMBAR

MYRTLE
UMBELLULARIA

MAGNOLIA
MAGNOLIA

RAISINTREE
HOVENIA

ZOO - WASHINGTON PARK ROAD

LEGEND
ROADS
PATHWAYS
PROPERTY LINES

MAPLE
ACER
COMMON NAME
BOTANICAL NAME

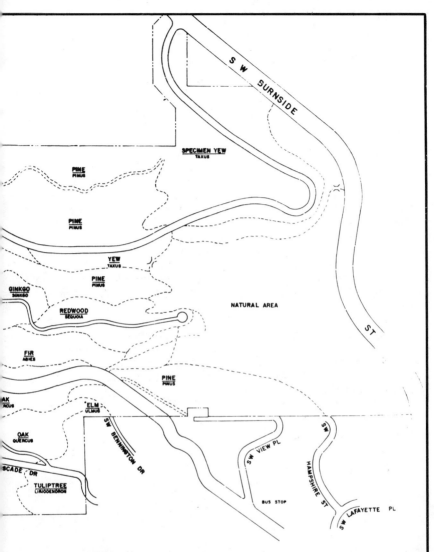

SW BURNSIDE

SPECIMEN YEW
TAXUS

PINE
PINUS

PINE
PINUS

YEW
TAXUS

PINE
PINUS

GINKGO
GINKGO

REDWOOD
SEQUOIA

NATURAL AREA

ST

FIR
ABIES

PINE
PINUS

AK
RCUS

ELM
ULMUS

OAK
QUERCUS

SW BENNINGTON DR

SW VIEW PL

SW HAMPSHIRE ST

SCADE DR

TULIPTREE
LIRIODENDRON

BUS STOP

SW LAFAYETTE PL

HOYT PARK ARBORETUM

CITY OF PORTLAND

BUREAU OF PARKS & RECREATION

0   50 100   200   300   400   500
SCALE IN FEET

1968 RG

FACILITIES

An attractive picnic shelter with a fireplace is located just off SW Fairview Blvd. on the west side. Across the street the old office building is being converted into a visitor's center, where you will be able to obtain maps and trail guides and see exhibits about the Arboretum. This building is also headquarters for an active volunteer program which provides tour guides and other support for the Arboretum.

TRAILS

SW Fairview Blvd. bisects the Arboretum and serves as a convenient dividing line between the coniferous and deciduous trees. The conifers and the *Redwood Tour Trail* are on the west side, the deciduous trees and the *Oak Tour Trail* on the east. Each of these trails is a 1-mile loop, starting near the parking lot on SW Fairview and winding gently up and down the hillsides. Self-guiding booklets are available for both trails, which are marked with numbered station posts. There is a viewpoint of the city and mountains just off the Oak Tour Trail close to the intersection of SW Fairview and Knights Blvd.

The 2-mile *Joggers' Loop* starts at the shelter, goes around the outside edge of the conifer area and back to the shelter.

A 3½ mile section of the *Wildwood Trail* winds through the Arboretum, making a connecting link with the Forestry Center area and the Japanese Gardens and Forest Park, as well as many other Arboretum trails.

A large detailed map updated in 1977 is available at the Arboretum office on SW Fairview Blvd. or the Park Bureau office downtown at SW 4th and Main.

JAPANESE GARDEN

Walking Distance	Less than a mile
Time to Spend	1 hour or more
Setting	Five distinct Japanese gardens: The Strolling Pond Garden The Tea Garden The Hillside-Moss Garden The Flat Garden The Sand and Stone Garden Natural forest background; distant views of the mountains
Distance from Downtown Portland	2 miles
Driving Directions	W on Burnside about ½ mile past 23rd Ave. to make a sharp L on SW Tichner and then a R on Kingston. Continue straight on Kingston, and park in the lot opposite the tennis courts. Follow the trail up the hill through the woods to the garden. (When the Zoo Train is running you can ride up, if you prefer.)
Bus	#62, Zoo/OMSI, and #76, Arlington, except on Sunday

The Portland Japanese Garden occupies the site of a former city zoo. Begun in 1962, the garden was built and is maintained by the Japanese Garden Society of Oregon, a private, nonprofit group. An admission charge supports their work. A brochure and a map with explanatory information about the five different garden styles are provided for visitors. The Garden is closed in the winter, and hours vary at other seasons, so call first to be sure they will be open when you wish to visit.

This is not the place to go for a hike, but rather for a delicate esthetic experience. These gardens are intended for contemplation, and a leisurely reflective mood is important for appreciating them.

Japanese gardens differ from both natural areas and Western gardens in several interesting ways: they provide an idealized symbolic conception of nature rather than a copy. Japanese gardeners choose predominantly green plants, believing that brilliant flowers detract from the peaceful effect desired. Evergreens are preferred so that the garden will be green all year round. In addition to green plants, essential elements of a Japanese garden include water, stones, paths, waterfalls, bridges, and sculptured ornaments. The gardens are designed to be beautiful from any perspective, and as you walk, new panoramas are constantly appearing.

HIMES PARK, JOHN'S LANDING, AND WILLAMETTE PARK

Walking Distance	5½ miles round trip
Time to Spend	½ day
Setting	Wooded canyon, urban riverfront
Distance from Downtown Portland	3½ miles
Driving Directions	S on SW Broadway to SW Terwilliger Blvd.; continue on Terwilliger to junction with SW Nebraska Street. Park here.
Bus	#46, Maplewood, goes past Himes Park on SW Terwilliger Blvd. #36, Oregon City-S. Shore, and #37, Oswego/Tualatin, go past John's Landing and Willamette Park along SW Macadam Ave.

HIMES PARK

If you want to find seclusion in deep woods close to home, Himes Park is one good place; we had the park to ourselves on a fine Sunday afternoon. It is best to come here in summer when the dense foliage absorbs much of the traffic noise.

A wide gravel path winds gently down into the canyon passing through a pleasant segment of second-growth conifer forest. The path continues under SW Barbur Blvd. and the freeway to emerge into a residential area at the junction of SW Iowa St. and SW Viewpoint Terrace (near Terwilliger School).

JOHN'S LANDING

From here you can follow sidewalks to the river at John's Landing. The asphalt walkway at the river's edge is a public path providing closeup views of the Willamette River and Ross Island, and there are usually sailboats and other river traffic to watch. You can walk north along the shore for about ½ mile, taking a dirt path after the pavement ends. This area is now a wasteland being prepared for new buildings (spring 78). Unfortunately all native vegetation has been removed except for a small stand of willows. Walking south, you pass the docks of John's Landing Yacht Club and the Willamette Sailing Club.

WILLAMETTE PARK

To get to Willamette Park, circumvent the chain link fence by walking up the fire lane and proceeding through the boat yard area to the park. Willamette Park is a Portland city park providing ½ mile of shoreline. There are picnic tables and large open fields perfect for flying kites.

It would be nice if this walk could be continued farther upstream along the Willamette to include Powers Marine Park, ¼ mile of riverfront under and south of the Sellwood Bridge. At present it is impossible for pedestrians to progress beyond the end of Willamette Park.

The disconnected riverfront trails at John's Landing and Willamette Park are part of Portland's contribution to the Willamette River Greenway. Depending on how far the Greenway plan is implemented in the future—currently a subject of debate—this detour may be eliminated. For more information on the Greenway in Portland, contact the City Planning Office.

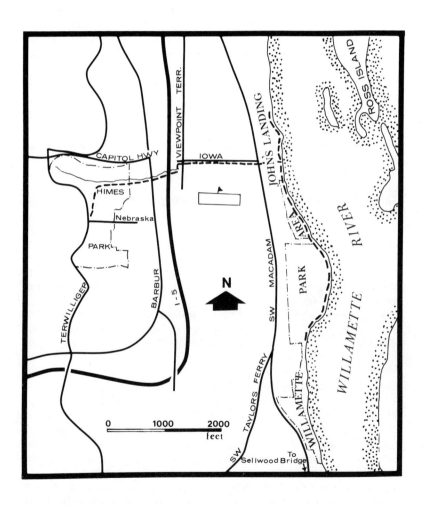

TERWILLIGER BIKE PATH AND EXERCISE COURSE

Walking Distance	**Bike Path,** 3½ miles one way from SW Barbur Blvd. to Duniway Park **Exercise Course,** 2 miles one way
Time to Spend	2-3 hours
Setting	Paved path through a fringe of parkland next to the road; scenic vistas
Distance from Downtown Portland	1 mile
Driving Directions	Drive S out of town on local streets. You can park at Duniway Park on Barbur Blvd., or if you want a shorter hike, at one of the turnoffs along SW Terwilliger Blvd.
Bus	Many bus lines go past Duniway Park on SW Barbur Blvd.: #s 1, 41, 42, 43, 44, 45, 55, and 56. #8, Sam Jackson Park, and #46, Maplewood, go up SW Terwilliger Blvd.

The idea for a scenic parkway along this wooded ridge above the city goes back to the 1904 "Park Plan" proposed by the Olmsted Brothers, renowned city planners who came to Portland to draw up plans for the 1905 Lewis & Clark Exposition. Begun in 1911, Terwilliger Blvd. was intended to provide a drive for "pleasure vehicles" which would take advantage of the fine vistas of the city, the river, and the mountains from the West Hills. In fact, the land was donated under the condition that the boulevard not be used for commercial vehicles. Construction of the bikeway has reinforced the role of Terwilliger Blvd. as a scenic parkway, but, on the other hand, traffic levels continue to rise, threatening to turn it into just another congested arterial.

Landslides have always been a problem here, because of the shallow topsoil underlain with an impermeable layer of clay. During construction of the hospital on Marquam Hill in 1921, a guard was posted on Terwilliger Blvd. to warn traffic in case of landslides. More recently, a section of the bike path slid down the hill soon after construction was completed.

BIKE PATH

The bike path, not yet crowded with cyclists, provides a pleasant place for walkers and joggers. There are nice vistas of the Willamette River and the east side of Portland, as well as the mountains in the background. This is a paved walkway parallel to a busy street, so the noise and smell of traffic detract somewhat from enjoyment of the woods and view. If you have the urge to penetrate deeper into these woods, take the trail down into the canyon at Himes Park (see Himes Park walk).

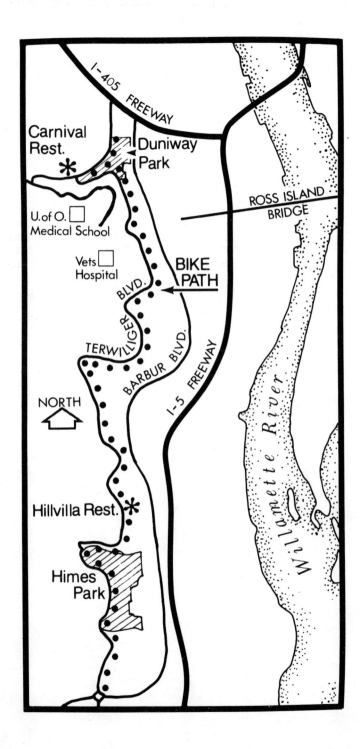

Carnival Rest.

I-405 FREEWAY

Duniway Park

U. of O. Medical School

Vets Hospital

BLVD.

TERWILLIGER

BARBUR BLVD.

BIKE PATH

ROSS ISLAND BRIDGE

I-5 FREEWAY

Willamette River

NORTH

Hillvilla Rest.

Himes Park

EXERCISE COURSE

The Exercise Course is modeled after the popular European *parcours*, which combines exercises with jogging. Twenty stations are located at one-tenth mile intervals in the woods just off the bike path. Each station has equipment and directions for a different exercise. This is an excellent place to bring a group of children who need to let off steam, as well as adults who want to get in condition!

REFUELING

If you want to stop for a meal during your walk, you can choose between two restaurants with unusual settings. Hillvilla is located at a high open spot along the Exercise Course, which provides sweeping views across the river. In the parking lot there is a public telescope (coin-fed) and an impressive totem pole. For more casual dining there is the Carnival Restaurant at the bottom of the hill at the end of the bike path. Here you can eat outdoors at a picnic table in a pretty grotto at the base of a cliff. If you are interested in geology, look up at the cliff from the parking lot to observe basalt columns.

COUNCIL CREST

Walking Distance	About 1 mile round trip
Time to Spend	1½ hours
Setting	Hilltop; open lawns and woods
Distance from Downtown Portland	3 miles
Driving Directions	S on SW Broadway, which becomes SW Broadway Dr. Continue uphill, following signs for Council Crest.
Bus	#51, Patrick Place, passes the bottom edge of the park.

Council Crest was named in commemoration of the traditional Indian use of the hilltop for council meetings. From 1907 to 1929 an amusement park operated here. An observation tower was provided, but the main attraction was the cable car which carried patrons up to the park from SW 18th Ave. and Spring St.

A city park today, Council Crest is well known for its imposing views, but most people don't realize that there are also walking trails available in the woods at the base of the butte. The best way to join up with the trail system is to start down the paved sidewalk leading to the microwave tower. Before you get to the fence around the tower, a well-used dirt trail takes off down the hill. The downhill trail ends at the junction of SW Talbot and SW Fairmont Streets. At this point lateral trails go off in either direction around the butte. Take your choice. Each eventually connects up with another trail bringing you back up to the manicured park area.

GABRIEL PARK

Walking Distance	1 mile
Time to Spend	45 minutes or more
Setting	Pretty natural woods; open fields of grass; manicured lawns
Distance from Downtown Portland	Don't drive across town, but if you live in the area, it's nice to know about the walking possibilities here.
Driving Directions	Turn N off SW Multnomah Blvd. onto SW 45th Ave. Park in the lot by the tennis courts on SW 45th.
Bus	#1, Mocks Crest/Vermont. Lines 42, 43, 45, and 46 go nearby.

Driving past this 90-acre neighborhood park, you have little indication that it provides anything more than typical park developments for mass recreation. However, there are two nice wooded areas for walking:

- From the parking lot, take the trail through the fringe of woods to the south between SW 45th and open fields.
- There are other nice trails along a small creek which bisects the park (where the street map indicates the right of way for SW Nevada Ave.).

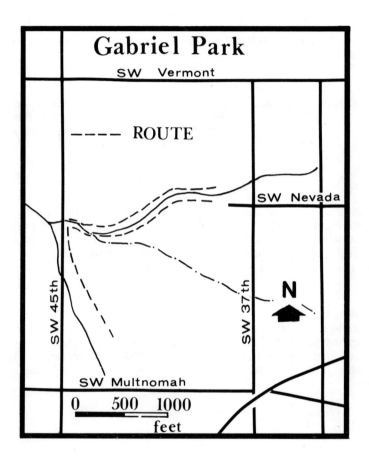

Gabriel Park

SW Vermont

- - - - ROUTE

SW Nevada

SW 45th

SW 37th

N

SW Multnomah

0   500   1000
feet

WOODS PARK

Walking Distance	¾ mile
Time to Spend	½ hour or more
Setting	Wooded ravine with stream; steep, sometimes muddy trails
Distance from	Don't drive across town for this, but if you
Distance from Downtown Portland	Don't drive across town for this, but if you live in this southwest area or shop along Barbur Blvd., you will be happy to discover it.
Driving Directions	Turn N off Barbur Blvd. onto SW Capitol Highway; turn L onto SW Brugger, then R onto SW Woods Parkway. The main area of the park lies between SW Woods Parkway and SW 45th Ave.
Bus	#s 41, 42, 43, and 44 go nearby.

This little-known county park is a delightful miniature wilderness near the congested commercial strip along Barbur Blvd. The park is undeveloped for the most part and little maintained, but there are restrooms, a small lawn, and a few fireplaces. We had the park to ourselves on a sunny weekend afternoon, though the area has obviously been used by neighborhood kids.

TRAILS

A network of trails descends to the bottom of the canyon and parallels the stream. Since these are use trails rather than engineered recreation trails, they are steep and muddy in places, and sometimes the trail along the stream side has eroded away. A walking stick is quite helpful.

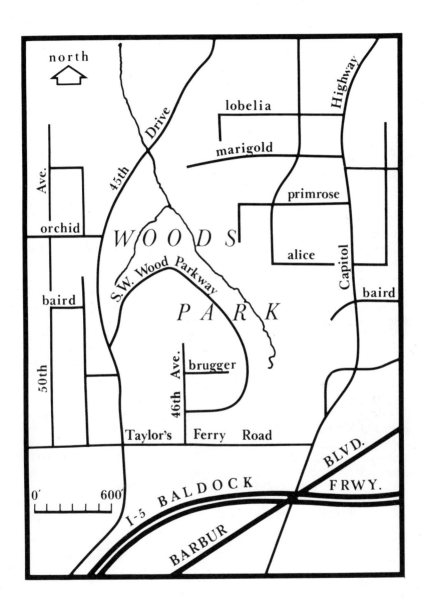

north

lobelia

marigold

Highway

45th Drive

Ave.

orchid

W O O D S

primrose

alice

Capitol

S.W. Wood Parkway

baird

baird

P A R K

50th

46th Ave.

brugger

Taylor's Ferry Road

0'   600'

I-5 BALDOCK

BLVD.

FRWY.

BARBUR

ELK ROCK GARDEN

Walking Distance	Approximately 1½ miles if you go on all trails
Time to Spend	1-2 hours
Setting	Panorama of the Willamette River including Elk Rock Island; garden containing a pleasing mixture of native and exotic plants in both semi-wild and manicured settings
Distance from Downtown Portland	5¾ miles
Driving Directions	S on SW Macadam Ave; turn L on Military Rd. and immediately R on SW Military Lane. Continue to the end of the road.
Bus	#36, Oregon City-S. Shore, and #37, Oswego/Tualatin, go along SW Macadam Ave.

Gravel trails wind back and forth along the hillside above a flat lawn. Botanical attractions include a large rhododendron area, a rock garden, mature yew trees, and a grove of madrones, unusual for our climate. Apparently they can flourish in the well-drained, rocky soil here. A small stream is another appealing feature.

This 13-acre estate, also known as the Bishop's Close, now belongs to the Episcopal Church, which allows public access to the garden.

This cliff, known as Elk Rock, is said to have gotten its name from local Indians who camped on the top. They made a practice of chasing animals off the cliff, descending later to retrieve them for food and clothing.

There are hair-raising stories about the railroad trestle which used to carry trains around the face of the cliff. The main problem was frequent rock falls from above. A guard from the railroad company would walk across the trestle before and after each train to clear off the rocks. But he was unable to prevent rocks from falling while a train was actually passing. These would sometimes go through the roof and "brain" a passenger. The trestle was eventually replaced by the present tunnel.

LEWIS & CLARK COLLEGE, PALATINE HILL WILD AREA, AND RIVERVIEW CEMETERY

Walking Distance **Jogging Trail,** 2½ miles when completed in fall 1978
Cemetery, up to 2 miles, round trip
Wild area, up to 2 miles, round trip, more if you get lost

Time to Spend **Campus,** 1 hour
Cemetery, 1 hour
Wild Area, ½ hour to ½ day

Setting College campus, wild area, manicured cemetery with sweeping views

Distance from Downtown Portland 5½ miles

Driving Directions S on I-5 to SW Terwilliger Blvd. exit; S on Terwilliger, following the sign at the road junction to the Lewis & Clark campus. Park in the college parking lot there at the N end of the campus (near the stadium.)

Bus Bus #40, Capitol Hill. Alternate buses on this line go to the campus or past the northern entrance to the cemetery. Lines #36, Maplewood, and #38, Wilsonville/ Mountain Park go near the cemetery. The wild area could be approached from the bottom (see below) by using buses which run on SW Macadam Ave., #36, Oswego/ Oregon City and #37, Oswego/Tualatin.

These three adjacent areas, which can be explored in the same day, provide sharply contrasting walking experiences.

LEWIS AND CLARK COLLEGE CAMPUS

The campus is the former Meier (of Meier & Frank) estate. The nicest part is the formal garden area behind the "Manor House." A series of terraces descends the hill behind the house. The various levels contain fountains, a reflecting pool, a rustic outdoor swimming pool among grape arbors, and, on the lowest level, the Lewis & Clark rose gardens. The grounds are a bit tacky, which only adds to the charm.

As we go to press, a jogging and exercise trail is being constructed around the edge of the campus. This is a Swedish-style jogging trail, with 20 exercise stations "designed for people who become bored jogging or running around a track." The trail goes around the south side of the campus and then through the woods at

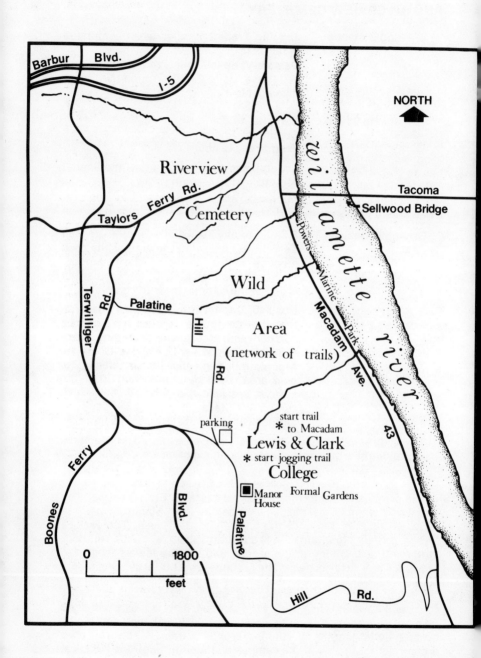

Barbur Blvd.

I-5

NORTH

Riverview

willamette river

Taylors Ferry Rd.

Cemetery

Tacoma

Sellwood Bridge

Wild

Terwilliger

Rd.

Palatine

Hill

Rd.

Area

(network of trails)

Powers Marine Park

Macadam Ave.

43

parking

*start trail
to Macadam

Lewis & Clark

* start jogging trail

College

Manor
House

Formal Gardens

Boones

Ferry

Blvd.

Palatine

0   1800

feet

Hill   Rd.

the south and west sides. You can connect with this trail in front of the chapel near the main gate. (Distinguish it from the other campus paths by the surface of bark dust.)

PALATINE HILL WILD AREA
Long Walk

This is a huge *de facto* wilderness, perhaps the most isolated area in the book. It is so little known that you are unlikely to meet another soul. A long walk in this wild area is not for the timid; much bushwhacking is involved, and there are many dead ends and impassable trails. It is the virtue of our climate that damaged areas, given a chance, are quickly covered with new growth, but this also means that little-used trails quickly become impenetrable.

There are many old trails and logging roads, but it is impossible to specifically identify most of them here. If you are lucky you can make a loop trip back to your starting point. Getting lost is a real possibility, though you could always follow the sound of traffic to a road.

There is one well-used trail from the northeast edge of the Lewis & Clark campus all the way down to SW Macadam Ave. (It emerges on Macadam near the "Speed 45" sign. From here you can cross Macadam and explore the Willamette riverfront in Powers Marine Park.) This trail is downhill all the way, muddy, and may be quite slippery, so perhaps it should be saved for a dry season. Another trail goes north from the same point along an old logging road overgrown with towering thimbleberry bushes. This one is easiest to traverse in winter. With perseverance, you can continue on it up to the developed part of the cemetery to the north.

Short Walk

Other entrances to this wild area are off SW Palatine Hill Rd. and from the northern edge of the Lewis & Clark parking lot. You can have a short walk in the woods here without getting seriously lost if you stay on the flat space, avoiding trails which go downhill. (The main trail downhill from here probably goes to SW Macadam Ave.)

RIVERVIEW CEMETERY

The developed part of the cemetery consists of open lawns sprinkled with a mix of native and ornamental trees and shrubs. As the name implies, there are nice vistas from here across the Willamette River to southeast Portland, and on clear days, beyond to Mt. Hood and Mt. St. Helen's. You can also catch glimpses of downtown through the trees. The best place for views is the open area at the southern entrance to the cemetery off SW Palatine Hill Rd.

The cemetery closes at 6 p.m.

You can get to the trails in the natural wooded area behind the developed part of the cemetery by going downhill from the mausoleum near the southern entrance gate beyond the cutaway hill.

PORTLAND COMMUNITY COLLEGE AND MT. SYLVANIA

Walking Distance	Campus, ¾ mile round trip Top of Mt. Sylvania, ¾ mile round trip (elevation 950 feet)
Time to Spend	1-3 hours
Setting	Campus: pavement; top of Mt. Sylvania: pavement or jeep trail (see below)
Distance from Downtown Portland	7 miles
Driving Directions	I-5 or SW Barbur Blvd. (99W) out of town to SW Capitol Highway exit. S on SW Capitol Highway which becomes SW 49th Ave.
Bus	#41, Portland Community College, and #78, Lake Oswego/Sunset (weekdays only)

Take a walk around the Portland Community College campus at Mt. Sylvania and see what your tax dollars have wrought. The spacious campus is a good example of the concrete-slab style of college architecture, which is softened somewhat by attractive plantings.

The primary principle of this community college is accessibility. All classes are on display, and it is fascinating to stroll along the outdoor aisles and peer into windows; you can see pots moulded, teeth cleaned, animals dissected. There is even a window labeled ''alchemy.''

Another principle of the college is to offer the utmost support to students, and a glance around the central mall shows this. Glass-fronted offices proclaim a wide variety of assistance: Information, Financial Aid, Math Help, English Help, Counseling. Students can look over the various helpers sitting behind the glass windows before deciding whether to utilize their services!

From the campus there are beautiful vistas of the hills and valleys to the west. This is a good place to watch cloud movements and sunsets, which are often spectacular, and the view is pretty at night when the many sparkling lights indicate that the area to the west is more heavily populated than it looks in the daytime.

Behind the campus, to the west, there is an undeveloped wooded area with use trails (bordered with luscious thimbleberries in July). The housing development to the west is encroaching, so that small natural area is probably doomed.

Mt. Sylvania itself (to the east of the PCC campus) is an extinct shield volcano responsible for much of the topography of the Southwest Portland-Lake Oswego area. The ''mountain'' was appropriately named for Silvanus, a Roman god who inhabited partly cleared woodlands on the fringe of civilization.

At the time of writing, it is still possible to walk along old jeep roads through the natural woods to the top, where there is a wide view in all directions. (Park your car at a turnoff on the east side of the road across from the college just before you get to the entrance.) But probably by the time you read this, the entire hillside will be covered with houses of the Mountain Park development, and Silvanus will have departed for good!

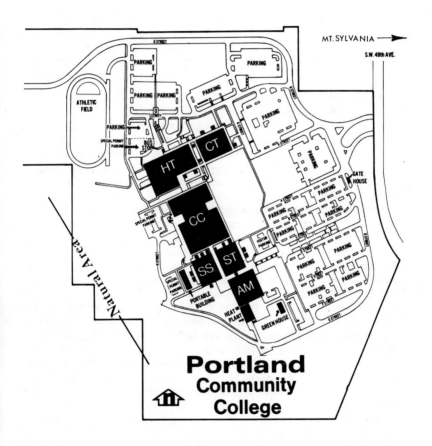

Portland
Community
College

TRYON CREEK STATE PARK

Walking Distance	7 miles of trails; many loop trips possible, short and long
Time to Spend	1-4 hours
Setting	Wooded canyons, small creek
Distance from Downtown Portland	6½ miles
Driving Directions	S on I-5 to Terwilliger exit; S 2½ miles on SW Terwilliger Blvd. and SW Terwilliger Extension to the park entrance.
Bus	#38, Wilsonville/Mt. Park, goes along the west side of the park on SW Boones Ferry Rd. during *weekday rush hours only.* (There is a trailhead on Boones Ferry Rd. which is about 1 mile from the Nature House.)

This 600-acre wilderness is a new kind of state park in Oregon—a natural site in an urban area. The primary impetus for creation of this park was preservation of the area. The state park sign at the entrance lists "trails" as the only recreation development here. There are no campgrounds, playgrounds, ball fields, fireplaces, or picnic tables. (Picnicking is allowed only in the shelter next to the Nature House.)

Because this park is managed to allow the natural cycles to occur with minimal interference from man, wildlife is abundant. More than 80 species of birds and numerous small mammals including beaver live in the park. In addition to the trees and shrubs common to second-growth forests, a large assortment of wildflowers, mushrooms, mosses, and lichens are found here. Trilliums are a special spring attraction.

The Nature House is the locus for information on the natural history of the area. Staffed by a full-time naturalist, the Nature House features interesting displays which change seasonally. There is an excellent reference library on Northwest natural history. On weekends orientation slide shows are presented, and the naturalist leads nature walks for the public. Throughout the week programs in environmental education are offered to school groups and other organizations.

Volunteers have recently prepared an attractive guidebook for the park: *Guide to an Urban Wilderness.* This book, on sale at the Nature House, contains detailed trail guides as well as identification keys and checklists for the flora and fauna of the park.

HISTORY

The existence of Tryon Creek State Park represents one of the great success stories of environmental action. The people in the area had long used and loved this wild canyon. With development in Portland and Lake Oswego encroaching on the area from three sides, it became clear that the site would not remain wilderness for long unless it could be preserved as a park.

In 1969 a citizens' group, Friends of Tryon Creek Park, was organized to help promote the creation of a park here. When 200 acres was optioned by a Seattle developer in 1970, an intense effort was begun to hold the area intact until sufficient funding could be found for a park encompassing most of the undeveloped land in the canyon. A community fund drive on the first Earth Day in April 1970 raised enough money for options on two endangered tracts of land.

In October 1970 an appeal to the State Highway Commission resulted in the crucial decision to establish a state park. The Friends of Tryon Creek worked with the state in creating a master plan for the park, which ensures that it will remain a natural area with minimal development. The trail system was built by 300 volunteers working by hand on one weekend in April 1973. The Friends also raised funds for the Nature House, which was completed in January 1975, and they continue to advise the State Parks Branch on operation of the park. They sponsor an active volunteer program. Volunteers perform many important tasks including leading guided nature walks for visiting school groups and garden clubs; helping the naturalist with exhibits, brochures, and other projects; staffing the information desk; and trail maintenance.

The primary human activity in this canyon in early days was logging, and observant visitors can see traces of the old logging roads and springboard notches in the old tree stumps. Logging began in 1880 when the timber here was used to produce charcoal for the iron furnace in Lake Oswego. (The remains of this furnace can still be seen in George Rogers Park in Lake Oswego.) Between 1912 and 1915 the area was logged again, and the lumber used for railroad ties and cordwood. During this period there was a logging mill along the creek, possibly in the area near Obie's Bridge. The last logging occurred in the north end of the park in 1961.

TRAILS

Come to Tryon Creek Park when you want to immerse yourself in the forest. Don't expect wide vistas or places to sit in the sun. It is always moist and shady here, and the trails are often muddy.

Three short flat loop trips of about ½ mile each are possible in the vicinity of the Nature House on the plateau above the creek. The Maple Ridge and Big Fir Loops are the most interesting.

Maple Ridge or North Loop

This very popular trail goes through the maple woods which has grown up since the climax cedar and hemlock forest was logged.

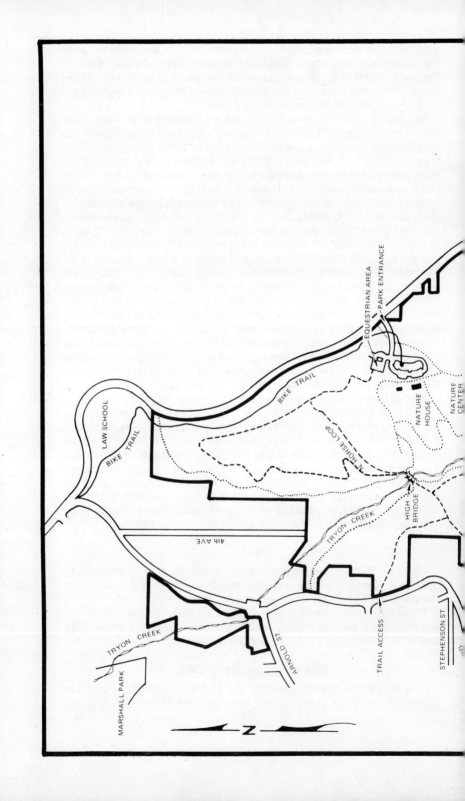

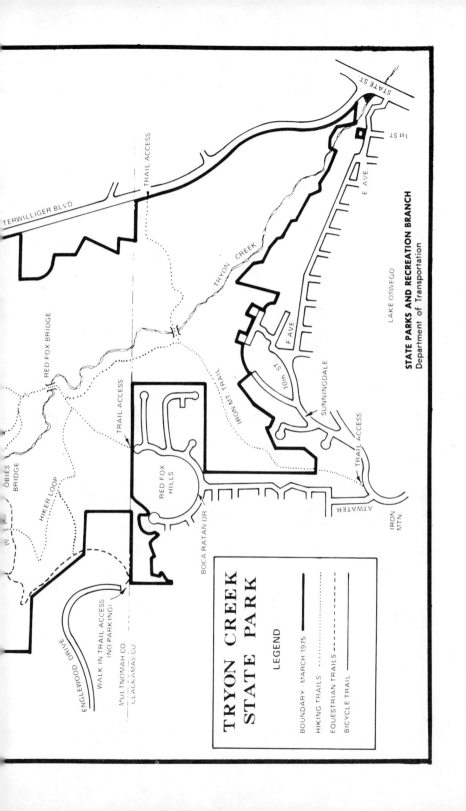

TRYON CREEK STATE PARK

LEGEND

BOUNDARY MARCH 1975 ——————
HIKING TRAILS ··············
EQUESTRIAN TRAILS – – – – –
BICYCLE TRAIL ——————

STATE PARKS AND RECREATION BRANCH
Department of Transportation

TERWILLIGER BLVD.

TRAIL ACCESS

STATE ST
1st ST
E AVE.
F AVE.
LAKE OSWEGO

TRYON CREEK

RED FOX BRIDGE
OBIES BRIDGE
HIKER LOOP
TRAIL ACCESS
RED FOX HILLS
IRON MT. TRAIL
BOCA RATAN DR.

10th ST
SUNNINGDALE
TRAIL ACCESS
ATWATER
IRON MTN.

ENGLEWOOD DRIVE
WALK IN TRAIL ACCESS (NO PARKING)
MULTNOMAH CO.
CLACKAMAS CO.

The outstanding feature of this trail is the huge gnarled old maple trees with trunks covered with moss and licorice fern. To find this trail, walk north from the Nature House past the shelter. To stay on the trail, take the left branch when the trail forks.

Big Fir Loop

This trail goes through an area of tall Douglas firs which miraculously has escaped logging in recent decades. To get to the Big Fir Loop, walk south from the Nature House along Old Main Trail.

A longer flat loop trip of 1.4 miles can be taken by combining the outer segments of these trails and the Center Loop Trail (see map). To stay on the circle, avoid all trails which go downhill.

Creek Loops

Most visitors to the park will want to see the creek, and it is easy to plot your own ''Creek Loop'' by looking at the map. These loops will be about 1¼ miles long, with an elevation drop of 125 feet.

The best views of the creek are from the bridges; the trail system was deliberately designed to avoid following close to the creek, to protect the fragile ecosystem along the banks. Please support this goal by staying on the trails.

You may notice air intakes for the sewer interceptor line which was built along the creek in 1965. This human intrusion had an unforeseen positive result: the wide swath that was cleared grew back in alder, providing a food supply for beaver who have returned to live in Tryon Creek since then. Beavers are nocturnal animals rarely seen by man, but observant visitors will notice signs of their activity.

We have described here only the most popular trails. If you want a solitary experience in the wilderness, avoid the area near the Nature House and explore the miles of other trails shown on the map (including the horse trails, which are open to hikers).

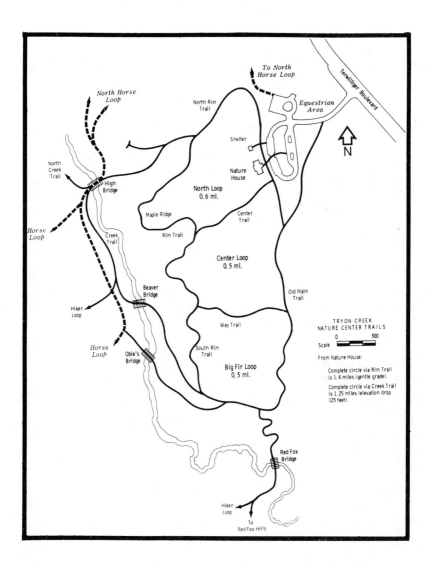

To North
Horse Loop

North Horse
Loop

North Rim
Trail

Equestrian
Area

Terwilliger Boulevard

Shelter

N

North
Creek
Trail

Nature
House

High
Bridge

North Loop
0.6 mi.

Maple Ridge

Center
Trail

Horse
Loop

Creek
Trail

Rim Trail

Center Loop
0.5 mi.

Beaver
Bridge

Old Main
Trail

Hiker
Loop

Way Trail

Horse
Loop

Obie's
Bridge

South Rim
Trail

Big Fir Loop
0.5 mi.

TRYON CREEK
NATURE CENTER TRAILS

0   300

Scale

From Nature House:

Complete circle via Rim Trail
is 1.4 miles (gentle grade).

Complete circle via Creek Trail
is 1.25 miles (elevation drop
125 feet).

Red Fox
Bridge

Hiker
Loop

To
Red Fox Hills

KELLEY POINT PARK

Walking Distance	2 miles
Time to Spend	2 hours or more
Setting	2 rivers and a slough; flood plain, sandy beach, cottonwood and willow woods
Distance from Downtown Portland	11½ miles
Driving Directions	I-5 to N Marine Drive exit; W on Marine Dr. to Suttle Rd. (just W of the Multnomah Expo Center); W on Suttle Rd. till it ends at the park.
Bus	No bus service

Kelley Point Park occupies a peninsula at the confluence of the Willamette and Columbia rivers in the northwest corner of the Rivergate Industrial District. It is the northern terminus of the Willamette River Greenway. The Port of Portland created this park by filling the watery peninsula with river dredgings. The Port states that "as Rivergate Industrial Area expands toward Kelley Point, it is planned that the two will be joined by a campuslike band containing office buildings and other low-key structures."

The special attraction of this park is its broad views: across the Columbia to the Washington shore, east to the Port of Portland's container-loading equipment, across the Willamette to Sauvie Island, south across the Columbia Slough to the Rivergate Industrial district. Humans seem dwarfed here, both by the magnificent rivers coming together and by the gigantic scale of the industrial installations. The passing river traffic is interesting to watch: from sailboats to tugboats to stately ocean-going vessels. Large waves created by the passing ships wash the shore.

The one defect of Kelley Point Park is the high noise level, from both the powerboats on the river and the nearby industrial areas.

A sandy beach stretches on either side of the point, and a gravel viewing area has been constructed at the point itself. The park also offers picnic tables among the cottonwood trees and a wide expanse of grass for sunbathing or games.

HISTORY

Kelley Point was named for Hall J. Kelley, an early promoter of the Oregon Territory in the 1830s, who dreamed of building a utopian metropolis on the site of the present Rivergate Industrial District. After various adventures he returned to Boston and died in poverty. Though his personal dream came to nought, his hard-sell enthusiasm inspired countless settlers to come to the Oregon Territory.

From 1895 to 1935 there was an octagonal Victorian lighthouse resting on pilings off the point. Unfortunately it was destroyed by fire. The site is still marked by the stubs of pilings.

WALK

For a 2-mile walk (as indicated on the map) start at the beach along the Columbia, round the point, proceed on the beach along the Willamette and then up the Columbia Slough. At the end of the sandy beach area along the slough, a use trail goes up along the bluff beside the slough, passing through a small abandoned orchard. When this trail becomes too overgrown for easy passage, use the old dirt road that parallels it a short distance inland. The road ends in a sandy expanse that is difficult to walk on. You can return to the developed part of the park along the dirt roadbed instead of retracing your course back to the beach. This road is a good place to see rabbits. The park is also home to heron, deer, beaver, and coyotes.

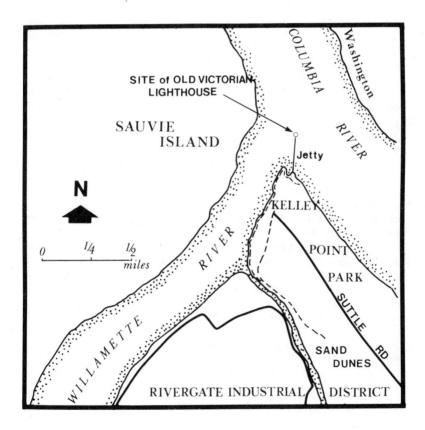

SITE of OLD VICTORIAN LIGHTHOUSE

SAUVIE ISLAND

COLUMBIA RIVER

Washington

Jetty

N

0   ¼   ½
miles

WILLAMETTE   RIVER

KELLEY POINT PARK

SUTTLE RD

SAND DUNES

RIVERGATE INDUSTRIAL   DISTRICT

ROCKY BUTTE

Walking Distance	1-4 miles round trip
Time to Spend	½ day
Setting	Wooded trails, flat or uphill; old quarry site; sweeping vistas from the top of the butte (see below)
Distance from Downtown Portland	6 miles
Driving Directions	E on NE Sandy Blvd., turn R onto NE Prescott; turn R again onto NE Maywood. There is good access to trails in the parklike area behind the junction of NE Maywood Place and NE Skidmore Street in the tiny community of Maywood Park.
Bus	#40, Halsey Fremont

Rocky Butte, well known as a jail site, also offers some nice hiking. Several trails take off from the wooded area behind the lawns. These approach trails (any one of which is as good as another) link up with a network of old roadbeds and motorcycle trails through the woods. (The whole area would be much pleasanter to walk in without the profusion of motorcycle roads, and there are new signs posted along NE Maywood Place prohibiting motorized vehicles.)

One very nice well-graded narrower trail switchbacks up the hill to Judson Bible College.

Other trails circle to the east around the butte past the site of the old quarry where prisoners were put to work in times past. This area is interesting geologically because it occupies a scour channel left by the Missoula Flood, and because the andesite which is the primary material composing the butte is exposed here. Several of the quarry pits have become ponds, with cattails and tadpoles.

Continuing south from here, it may be possible to go by trail or motorcycle from the area behind the jail up to the observation area area at the top of the butte. (We challenge you to find a route! We didn't.) In any case the observation area is well worth a visit, by foot or by car, for the sweeping vistas it offers in all directions. The massive fortlike structure (which we mistook for the jail at first) is popular with kids. Unfortunately this park area is poorly maintained; garbage abounds, and the "fort" is disfigured with paint.

There is reputed to be a grove of quaking aspen on the north side of Rocky Butte—something else we couldn't find!

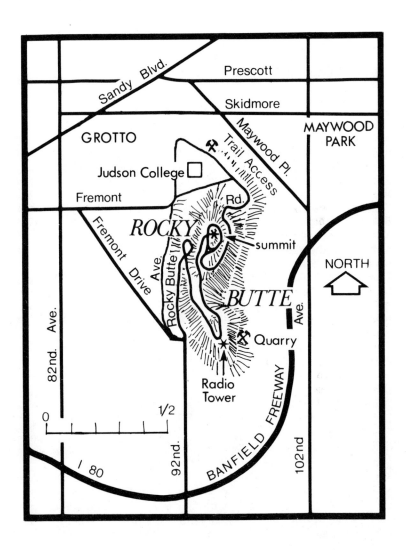

Sandy Blvd.

Prescott

Skidmore

GROTTO

MAYWOOD PARK

Maywood Pl.

Judson College

Trail Access

Fremont

Rd.

ROCKY

summit

NORTH

Fremont Drive Ave.

Rocky Butte Ave.

BUTTE

102nd Ave.

Quarry

82nd. Ave.

Radio Tower

0   1/2

92nd.

I 80

BANFIELD FREEWAY

DELTA PARK

Walking Distance	Any distance up to 5 miles
Time to Spend	2 hours or more
Setting	Open flood plain, overgrown slough
Distance from Downtown Portland	6 miles
Driving Directions	N on I-5 to Delta Park exit.
Bus	#6, Union Ave., goes along the northern edge of East Delta Park.

East and West Delta Parks (on the east and west sides of I-5) provide a huge open space—a good place to come if walks in the woods induce claustrophobia! This is a fine location for birdwatching, plane spotting, kite flying, letting your dog run. Recreations which require a lot of space happen here, and much of the fun of walking here lies in wandering around observing them.

East Delta Park has a helicopter landing field, a model airplane field, and athletic fields. There are picnic tables beside a pond and a children's playground. Portland Meadows Race Track is at the south end, and in the stable area beyond the racetrack, you can watch the horses being exercised.

West Delta Park is much larger, containing a municipal golf course (with a snack shop in the clubhouse) and Portland International Raceway. The purpose of the track is "to give people a place to use their vehicles safely." This applies to any vehicles with wheels, from bicycles to dragsters.

This section of the park also includes some nice "wasteland" bordering the Columbia Slough. There are many long narrow ponds lined with brush, making a hospitable habitat for birds. We saw a pheasant here.

HISTORY

This recreation site has an unusual history. The barren expanse of land was once the home of 40,000 people. During World War II the instant city of Vanport was erected here to house workers in the Kaiser shipyards. Construction was started in September 1942, and by mid-December almost 10,000 housing units had been completed. Vanport was a complete city, with four major shopping centers and schools. Within a year the population was 40,000, making it the second biggest city in Oregon and the largest war-housing town in the United States.

The city was completely wiped out by a disastrous flood on Memorial Day, 1948. There had been an unusually heavy snowpack that winter and three times the normal rainfall. The system of dikes built by the Army Corps of Engineers in 1941 to protect the area broke without warning, and the whole city was flooded in 90 minutes, leaving 18,500 people homeless. Miraculously, fewer than 20 people died. A wise decision was made not to rebuild the city in such a flood-prone location, and the area is now more appropriately reserved for recreation.

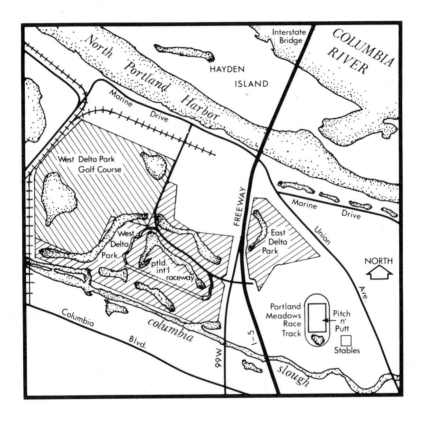

PIER PARK

Walking Distance	1 mile or more
Time to Spend	1½ hours
Setting	Stately groves of mature conifers on open lawn
Distance from Downtown Portland	9 miles
Driving Directions	Take I-5 N to N Lombard St. exit; go W and then N on Lombard, then N on St. John's Ave. to the park.
Bus	#2, St. John's, goes on N. Lombard St.

Pier Park is unusual among Portland city parks for the maturity and variety of its trees. Containing many kinds of conifers (including redwood as well as broad-leaf trees such as paper birches), this park resembles an arboretum. The scent of the fir needles accumulated on the ground adds to the forest atmosphere.

Though there are asphalt trails, you can walk anywhere because the understory which would naturally grow in such a forest has been cleared.

Contrary to the impression given by its name, Pier Park is *not* a waterfront park.

This park is a popular place for group picnics on weekends.

SANDY RIVER I: Oxbow Park

Walking Distance	7 miles or less. It is a walk of at least 3 miles along the shore from the east end of the park to the western boundary at Camp Collins. If you come down from above, add at least another ½ mile (and 700 feet of elevation change). Thus a complete round trip would be 7 miles.
Setting	Forested river shore with some sandy areas and some rocky areas.
Time to Spend	1 day
Distance from Downtown Portland	About 20 miles
Driving Directions	E on Highway 26 (SE Powell Blvd.) to SE Orient Dr. SE Orient to SE 282nd St., N to SE Lusted Rd. Turn N (L) on Hosner Rd., which becomes the entrance road to the park. If you are **not** planning to hike down to the gorge (see description below) you can take this road down to the park at the river level. If you do want to hike down, turn right at the next intersection onto Homan Rd. Continue straight on Homan until it dead-ends, and park there.
Bus	No bus service.

The Sandy River Gorge is an amazing natural area very close to Portland. Thanks to the Nature Conservancy, almost all of the shore between Oxbow Park and Dodge Park is now protected from development. Since 1972 they have been accumulating, through donations and purchases, the private lands remaining in the gorge.

An astonishing variety of wildlife is still reported in the gorge. Interesting mammals include deer, coyote, raccoon, muskrat, mink, beaver, opossum, and porcupine. Even bear, elk, and cougar have been spotted. Observant birdwatchers have seen osprey, pileated woodpeckers, three species of owl, great blue heron, mergansers, ruffled grouse, and belted kingfishers.

This large county park with several miles of hiking trails is our favorite locale for hiking on crisp winter days. The park, which is swamped with picnickers on hot summer days, is virtually deserted in winter. (Even in summer, the upper area is quite empty.)

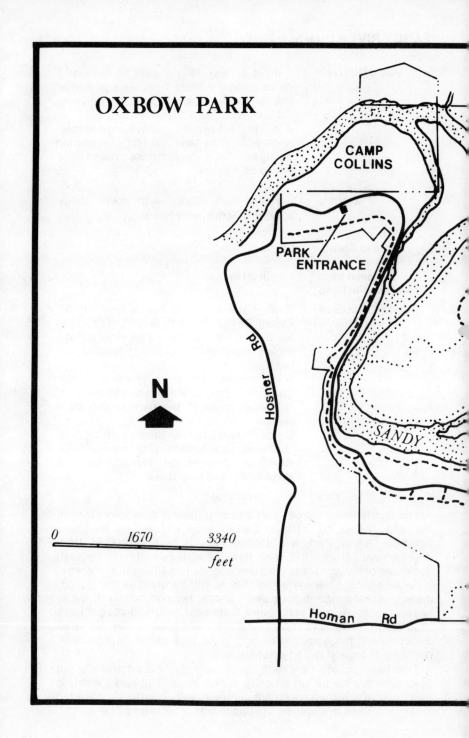

OXBOW PARK

CAMP COLLINS

PARK ENTRANCE

Hosner Rd

SANDY

N

0   1670   3340
feet

Homan Rd

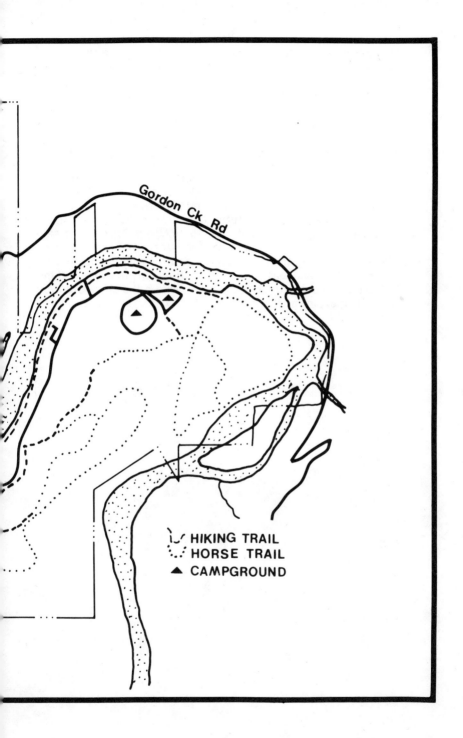

Gordon Ck Rd

⌣ HIKING TRAIL
⋰ HORSE TRAIL
▲ CAMPGROUND

TRAILS

The entrance road to the park takes you down to the river level, but it is much nicer to hike down by trail. Park at the end of Homan Rd. (See Driving Directions above.) Here you are 700 feet above the river. Before descending, you can enjoy a nice view of Mt. Hood across the Sandy Gorge. There are many use trails dropping down to the small flood plain. Some are steeper than others, but a fairly gentle route can be found. It's impossible to indicate a specific route among the network of trails—just keep going down. (If the trail becomes too steep for your taste, backtrack till you find a gentler trail.) At the bottom of the gorge you emerge at the road through the park. Cross the road and proceed to the water's edge where you will find more trails paralleling the river in either direction.

To make a loop trip to return to your car, follow the river downstream through the park till you get to Camp Collins (a private YMCA camp bordering Oxbow Park). From there you can walk back up the entrance road to your starting point. Less ambitious people can take two cars and leave one at the bottom. Or, to avoid walking in the road, you can retrace your steps back up the cliff, after you have finished exploring the trails along the shore.

SANDY RIVER II: Dabney State Park

Walking Distance	1½ - 2 miles round trip
Time to Spend	About 2 hours
Setting	Wooded shore
Distance from Downtown Portland	About 15 miles
Driving Directions	Highway 80N east to Lewis and Clark State Park exit. Go S past the park and Troutdale Bridge following the Scenic Highway. Dabney State Park is on the right about ½ mile beyond the Stark Street Bridge.
Bus	No bus service

This park is well known for water activities—wading, swimming, and rafting. However, it is also nice for hiking. Because the park is very popular with teenagers (particularly those with noisy vehicles) it's better to come in off-seasons if you want privacy and a feeling of isolation. In winter only a few fishermen are here.

TRAILS

Trails parallel the river for the length of the park. Though you can intersect the riverside trails at many points, we will recommend one: Drive to the last parking lot to the east. Follow a gravel trail to the end, then descend steeply to the river. Take trails east or west, up or downstream. The trail upstream (east) continues to a large boulder on the edge of the river which marks the eastern boundary of the park. Near here a creek with two falls comes down off the cliff. This creek cuts a narrow canyon which forms a sharp, steep ridge. For those who like a challenge, a "trail" climbs up the edge of the ridge to a point near a road junction at Springville.

You can also walk downstream along any one of a network of trails which go through the woods between the river and the cliff. Depending on the water level, in places you can walk along the rocks in the open instead. Sandy patches good for sunbathing occur here and there along the shore.

SANDY RIVER III: Sandy River Delta

Walking Distance	4-6 miles. Round trip out to the junction of the Columbia and Sandy Rivers is about 4 miles. Total distance will depend upon which routes you choose, and how far you want to walk along the shore of the Columbia.
Time to Spend	½ to 1 day
Setting	Flat Columbia River flood plain, pasture, sandy beach, and brushy areas. Mostly open with sweeping vistas.
Distance from Downtown Portland	About 15 miles
Driving Directions	Highway 80 N East to Lewis and Clark State Park exit. Park near the motorcycle park.
Bus	#18 Troutdale (No Sunday service)

Lewis and Clark, passing the mouth of the Sandy River in November 1805, noted that "this river throws out immense quantities of sand . . . [and] on attempting to wade across we discovered that the bed was a very bad quicksand." They named it "Quicksand River," which was later shortened by usage to "Sandy River."

The origin of the river in the Ramona Glacier on Mt. Hood accounts for the cloudy water in summer. Glacial melt waters contain "glacial flour," ground-up particles of rock. (This is a good reason not to drink the water.)

The river is noted for smelt runs which occur unpredictably in the early spring of some years. When they come, the shores of the lower river take on a festival aspect with hundreds of people of all ages dipping up their 20-pound daily limit in a few minutes. This natural largesse is a fine source of free protein.

Chances of being alone are good at the mouth of the Sandy, but you won't be able to forget civilization completely. There is the noise of the freeway, of planes coming in for a landing at Troutdale Airport, and of motorcyclists in the newly created county motorcycle park between the freeway and Lewis and Clark State Park. The noise diminishes a good deal as you get closer to the Columbia, but then your nose may be assaulted by the fumes from the pulp mill at Camas.

However, these defects are balanced by the attractions of sandy beaches and wide vistas up, down, and across the Columbia River.

For bird lovers there are herons, hawks, and numerous smaller birds.

Be sure to take water with you. This can turn out to be a long hike, most of it in the open, and there is no safe natural source of water.

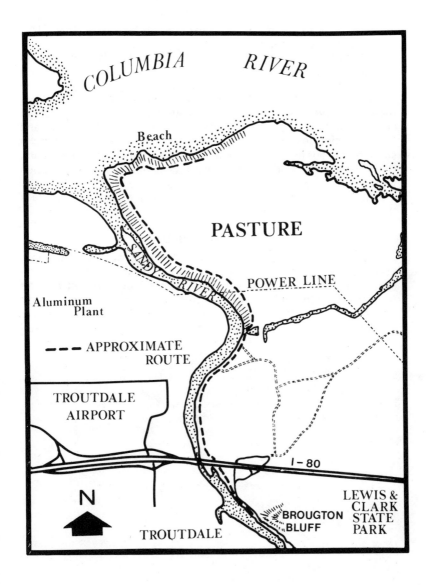

WALK

Begin the walk by descending to the shore. Then make your way west to the Columbia by whichever route seems best at the time. We can't recommend a specific trail as the terrain changes frequently due to shifting water levels, and the route you choose will depend somewhat on whether or not you want to wade. You can judge approximately how far you have come by the landmarks of the inlet and the powerlines. After passing the inlet, it should be easy to locate a cow trail along the bluff overlooking the Sandy River. This will take you to the specific point where the Sandy and Columbia join. As you approach the Columbia, the trail passes an area of beaver activity among a fringe of willows between the pasture and the shore.

To descend to the long stretch of beach along the Columbia from here you have two choices: Fight your way through a patch of stinging nettles, or detour partway back into the cow pasture and find an easier descent. This is a lovely beach, perfect for wading or sunbathing, but beware of the quicksand encountered by Lewis and Clark! (We didn't find it.) The beach was completely deserted when we were there.

You can return the way you came or find a different route back through the pasture.

BROUGHTON BLUFF

Before or after this hike, you may wish to stop at Lewis and Clark State Park to scramble up Broughton Bluff, a formation of mudstone capped with 100 feet of lava. Several "trails" up the bluff take off from the camping area at the east end of the park. These trails go *very* steeply up without switchbacks and are only recommended for adventurers. In fact, a sign in front of the well-worn main trail states: "Warning. Unstable Rock Dangerous to Climbers."

LEACH PARK GARDEN

Walking Distance	½ mile
Time to Spend	¾ hour, more if you are interested in botany or horticulture
Setting	Dense woods containing both native and exotic plants in a natural setting.
Distance from Downtown Portland	9 miles
Driving Directions	E on SE Powell Blvd. to SE 50th; R here on SE Foster Rd. Continue on Foster to SE 122nd Ave. and turn R. The garden is on the L just before the bridge. A sign over the gate reads "Sleepy Hollow."
Bus	#26, Holgate/33rd Ave., and #14, 52nd Ave. Lincoln Memorial

NOTE: Advance reservations must be made 2 weeks ahead through Portland Park Bureau. Weekends are the preferred time for visiting.

This charming old estate obviously belonged to a family with an intense interest in horticulture. Like Elk Rock Garden or the Japanese Garden, the attraction of this garden is its special mood, rather than the extent of its trails. Because of the necessity of planning visits in advance, you are unlikely to have the mood disturbed by the presence of other visitors.

The most enticing area is below the entrance road where rustic trails lead down to a sylvan scene beside Johnson Creek. A perfect setting for 19th Century romantic poets; it would be easy to believe in fairies here.

There is also a maze of trails through interesting plantings above the road.

MT. TABOR

Walking Distance	2 miles round trip
Time to Spend	1½-2 hours
Setting	Panoramic views of the city and surrounding countryside; exposed crater, reservoirs, groves of large old trees and plantings of native trees and shrubs.
Distance from Downtown Portland	3 miles
Driving Directions	E on SE Stark to SE 60th; R (S) onto SE Salmon; E on Salmon into park. (There is another entrance at SE 69th and Belmont.) To find the trails, park at the crater.
Bus	#21, Mt. Tabor

It is easy to drive the winding road to the top of Mt. Tabor, look at the view from your car, and drive home without realizing that this is also a good place for walking. Following the footpaths that spiral down from left of the crater, you can better savor the changing vistas, besides getting a closer look at the crater and the reservoirs.

Portland Park Bureau release #3003 provides some interesting geological information about Mt. Tabor:

Excavations carried on during development work in the park in 1912 exposed the cinder and rock of the old crater. Cinders were being used in surfacing paths and drives in the park, and the interesting lava rock for construction of rockeries and other landscape details, when geologists discovered the historical significance of the cut which exposed core and throat of the cinder cone. It was their theory that this cinder cone is evidence of a one-time fiery blow-out and that the Mt. Tabor volcano breathed its hot gases and spewed its pyrotechnical displays even before Mt. Hood was formed.

In the cross-cut of the west wall of the bowl may be seen beds of the material that fell out of the crater sloping to the north and south away from the center. Beds of material that fell inside the crater slope westward toward its center. Near the top is a lens of yellowish brown, the burnt gravels that were thrown up by some extra violent explosions but which fell back within the crater. The easterly wall of the cut shows cinder beds sloping to the north, the east, and the south away from the crater.

The four large reservoirs hold water from Bull Run for the city's domestic water supply. In summer, plumes of water shoot up for aeration purposes.

Portland's Mt. Tabor was named for the biblical Mt. Tabor in Palestine by Plympton Kelly, a pioneer settled, who homesteaded on neighboring Kelly Butte, also an interesting hill to explore on foot.

Mt. Tabor Park has playground and picnic facilities. On warm summer evenings it is a major congregating point for the young people in the area, and traffic noise can be quite distracting.

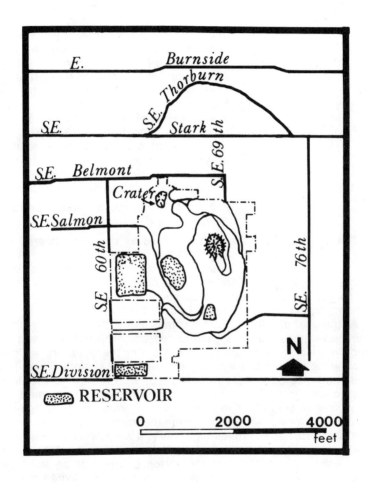

KELLY BUTTE

Walking Distance	About 1 mile
Time to Spend	About 2 hours
Setting	Steep ascent through woods and brush to good views from the top (elevation 577 feet); peaceful and mostly undeveloped.
Distance from Downtown Portland	5 miles
Driving Directions	E on SE Division. There are many approaches to Kelly Butte. **If you want to climb up to the top of the butte by trail,** turn R (S) off Division onto SE 101 St. Drive a couple of blocks to the end of the road where the trail will be visible (see below). **If you just want to walk around on top,** turn R (S) off Division onto SE 103rd and follow it to the end. The paved road stops at the tower installation. A dirt road continues, which may be blocked to cars by a gate but is accessible to walkers.
Bus	#19, East Glisan, going **toward** downtown Portland and #9, Powell

The view from the top isn't as grand as it is from nearby Mt. Tabor, but the undeveloped part of Kelly Butte is more tranquil and natural. Actually it is amazing to discover a natural area at all between the busy commercial arteries of SE Powell and SE Division. Of course the butte won't be so peaceful when I-205, now being constructed, cuts across the west side of it.

At the west end there is a water tank and at the east end a police communications center sprouting red and white towers from an underground installation. The shoulders of the butte are wooded, but the top is quite brushy, with occasional viewpoints. There is at least one nice open field near the top, with a view to the south toward Mt. Scott. From the area above the water tank there is a good view west to Mt. Tabor and beyond across the Willamette. In winter you can also see north through the trees.

Kelly Butte has an interesting history. It was named for Plympton Kelly, an early homesteader. Kelly Butte was the site of the county jail in the early 1900s, and the prison quarry was an important source of rock for the construction of county roads. When the rock was pretty well quarried out, the county purchased the present jail site on Rocky Butte, and today the police communications center occupies the excavated area.

TRAILS

The trail to the top from SE 101 St. is fairly steep and may be muddy. (From the paved parking area, a gravel trail equally steep leads directly to the water tank.) From the old roadbed on top, numerous inviting side trails take off into the woods.

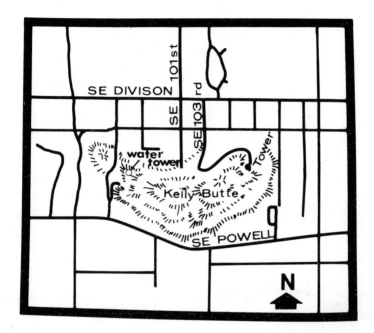

OAKS BOTTOM

Walking Distance	About 3 miles round trip
Time to Spend	2 hours
Setting	Flat marsh covered with cottonwoods and willows; shore of Willamette River
Distance from Downtown Portland	5¾ miles
Driving Directions	S on 99E to SE Tacoma St.; R (W) on SE Tacoma to SE 7th Ave.; R (N) on SE 7th to Sellwood Park
Bus	No good service

ECOLOGY

Oaks Bottom represents a remnant of the Willamette Valley flood plain within the Portland city limits. Composed of silt deposits left by the Willamette River, the wetland is enclosed by higher land: a bluff 80-100 feet high on the east and the (artificial) railroad embankment on the west.

Periodic flooding is an important ecological factor here. Since the elevation is only 5 to 15 feet above the Willamette, the entire area will be several feet under water at least once every five years. This flooding discourages nesting waterfowl, and it has been suggested that the water level could easily be stabilized by the installation of a water control gate at the culvert that passes through the railroad fill (which acts as a dike). A policy question is raised here which applies to many of the places in this book: Should a site be managed to attract more wildlife or left to develop as "nature" determines?

Flooding is dependent on fluctuations in rainfall and riverflow, but the area is always wet because it is fed by several year-round springs from the Crystal Springs system, which originate at the base of the bluff along the eastern edge of the wetlands. These streams eventually join in the bottom and flow on to the river.

Cottonwood and willow are the dominant tree species in the bottom. (There are few, if any, oaks here now.) Because these are deciduous trees, in winter the area is quite barren—some would say dreary. Along the bluff is a different vegetation including swamp ash, big leaf maple, blackberry, Scotch broom, horsetail, and grasses.

Oaks Bottom has been identified by naturalists as the best wildlife habitat in the Portland area. Thanks to a fortuitous combination of food, water, cover, size, and isolation from man, the location supports many different species of birds, reptiles, and mammals. Especially impressive are the great blue herons resident on Ross Island who come to the bottom to feed. Some species such as hawks, eagles, and deer have been driven out by the high noise levels.

In addition to the wetlands, the riverfront itself constitutes another very important wildlife habitat. The overhung banks and fringe of woods provide food and shelter for many riparian animals. The shallow channel between Oaks Bottom and Hardtack Island is an important warm water fish-producing area. There are fill areas to the north and south of the wetlands (see map). The natural vegetation has been destroyed in these areas by the filling and by illegal motorcycle use, but grass, bushes, and small trees are beginning to come back, creating a distinct new wildlife habitat. The railroad embankment in the north fill zone makes a good vantage point for birdwatching because the top of it is level with the treetops.

PRESERVATION

Oaks Bottom, like Forest Park, has been a *de facto* wilderness, which has lately come to be recognized as a valuable natural resource in our urban area. In the last few years local people have become worried that unless the area was given formal protected status, the wildlife population and habitat would be destroyed by illegal motorcycle use and development on adjacent private property.

Oaks Bottom has been quite intensively studied in the effort to determine the best future for the area. Two useful reports are available at the Multnomah County Library:

McCoy, Michael, *Oaks Bottom: Planning a Natural Park in Portland,* Report of the Sellwood-Moreland Improvement League, 9/21/73.

Kerr, Donald M., *Wildlife in Oaks Pioneer Park,* Report prepared for Children's Museum, Portland Park Bureau.

The Sellwood-Moreland Improvement League, the Portland Audubon Society, and the Portland Park Bureau have collaborated to save the area, which is now part of the Portland park system. Trails were constructed by volunteers in the summer of 1976, and the Audubon Society has been conducting educational activities and habitat improvement.

TRAILS

To descend from Sellwood Park to Oaks Bottom, go to the northeast corner of the park and find the wide gravel trail (which was labeled when we were there). This is a sturdy elevated trail, dry most of the time. It follows the base of the bluff, an interesting border, or ecotone, between the wetlands and the woods, and ends in a gravel road which goes up to Milwaukie Ave. at the north end of Oaks Bottom. Two lesser trails cross the north fill to the waterfront (see map). Unfortunately there is no good trail along the waterfront itself, though you can pick your way along the railroad track.

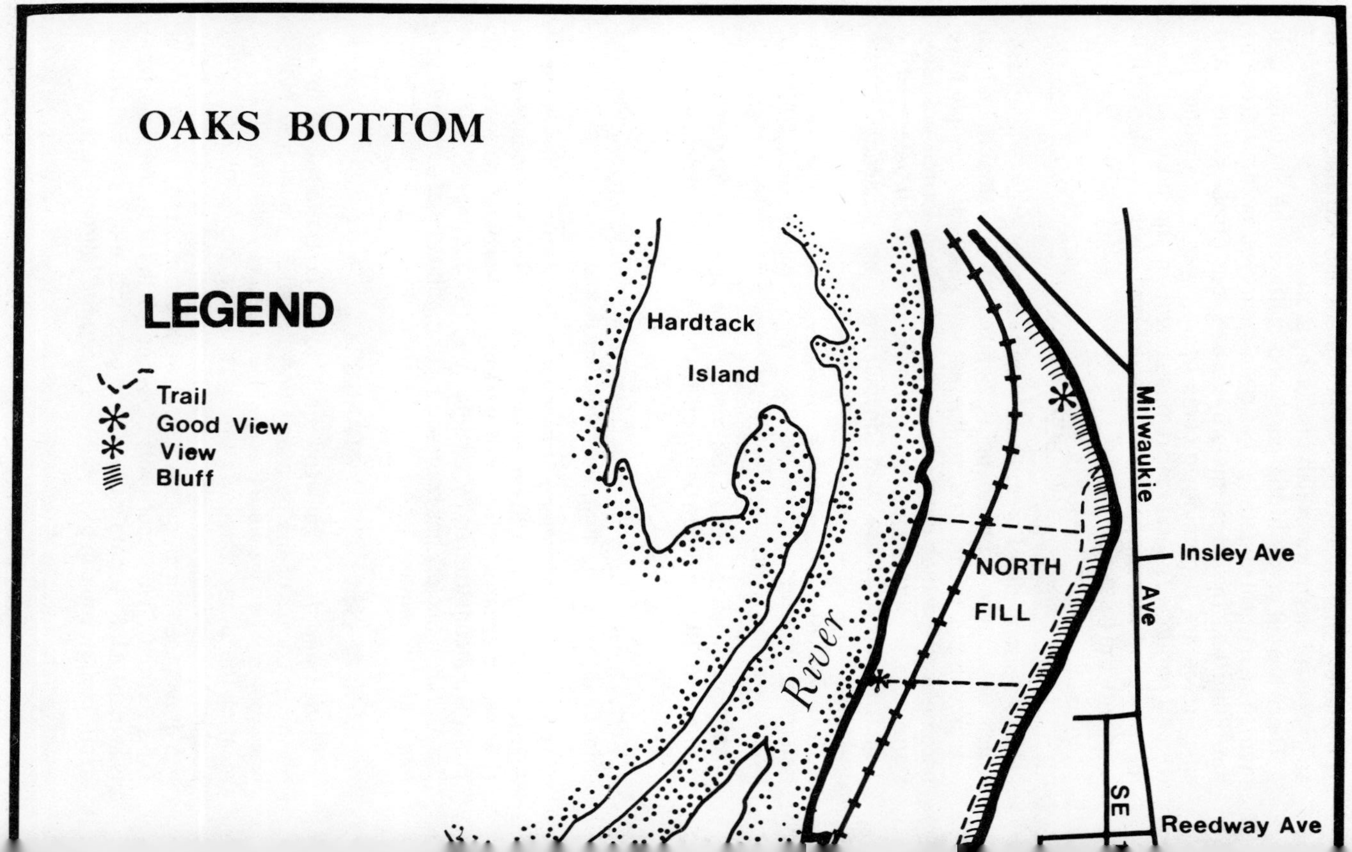

OAKS BOTTOM

LEGEND

Trail   ⌣

Good View   ✳

View   ✳

Bluff   ▥

Milwaukie Ave

Insley Ave

Reedway Ave

SE

NORTH FILL

River

Hardtack Island

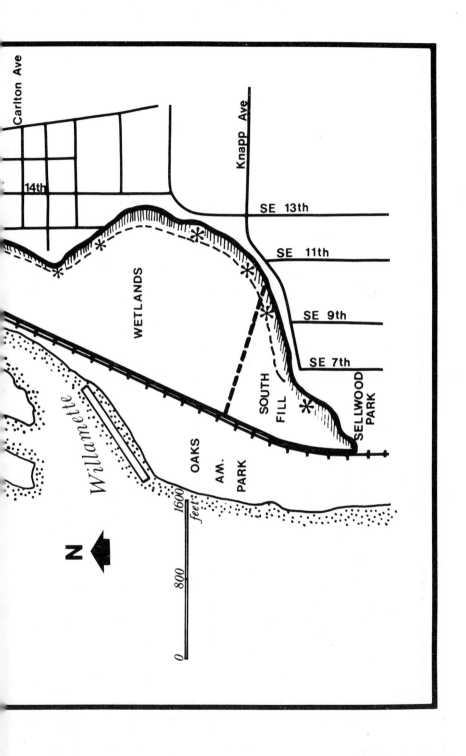

CRYSTAL SPRINGS CREEK

Walking Distance	3¾ miles one way; for a shorter trip, any of the 4 sections can easily be taken separately.
Time to Spend	½ to 1 day
Setting	Creek, swamp, ponds, Rhododendron Garden, city streets
Distance from Downtown Portland	4¼ miles
Driving Directions	E on SE Powell Blvd. (US 26) to SE 39th Ave.; turn R (S) on SE 39th; turn R (W) on SE Reedway and park where you can along the road.
Bus	#28, Eastmoreland, and #27, Harold, go to Reed; #30, Ardenwald, #31, Estacada, and #33, Oregon City, go past Westmoreland Park on SE McLoughlin Blvd.

This 3¾-mile walk follows the course of Crystal Springs Creek from its origin on the Reed College campus to the point where it flows into Johnson Creek. The trek takes you through four locations, each attractive in a different way: Reed Lake, the Rhododendron Garden, Westmoreland Park, and Johnson Creek Park. The walk can be followed in either direction, but we prefer to go downstream.

REED LAKE

Begin your hike by taking the footpath at the west end of SE Reedway. There are several trails here. Keep going downhill and follow the sound of falling water to the clear spring which is the source of water for the stream and lake beyond. Continue along the stream, preferably on the south side, through very lush swamp growth. Primitive side trails lead to secluded nooks in the swamp. Giant skunk cabbage, mossy trees, and the calls of many kinds of birds create a tropical mood. All these trails may be very muddy and slippery. Keep walking downstream, past the stream outlet and along the lakeshore. Trails along both shores are joined by a unique red and yellow foot bridge supported by only two posts, one on each shore. There is a rustic outdoor amphitheatre on the south shore of this small lake.

The trail continues downstream beyond the lake to a theater built over the stream. The woods beyond the theater are impenetrable, so climb up to the road here.

To proceed to the Rhododendron Garden, follow the campus road down to 28th Ave. and cross the street.

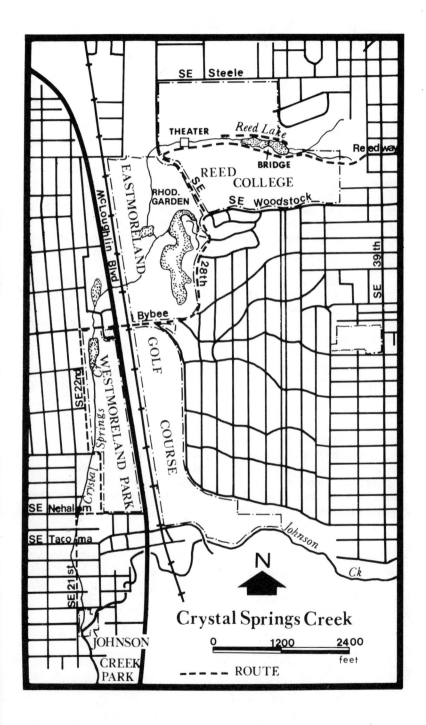

SE Steele

THEATER Reed Lake

Reedway

REED
COLLEGE

BRIDGE

EASTMORELAND

RHOD.
GARDEN

SE Woodstock

McLoughlin Blvd

SE 39th

28th

Bybee

GOLF

WESTMORELAND PARK

SE22nd

Crystal Springs Ck

COURSE

SE Nehalem

SE Taco ma

Johnson

SE 21st

Ck

N

Crystal Springs Creek

0   1200   2400
feet

JOHNSON

CREEK
PARK

----- ROUTE

RHODODENDRON GARDEN

Crystal Springs Rhododendron Garden is a city park developed and maintained by the Portland chapter of the American Rhododendron Society and the Portland Park Bureau. The park contains seven acres of woodland with 2,500 rhododendron plants (and samples of other interesting shrubs and trees) planted along almost a mile of pathways. The Rhododendron Society has prepared an attractive brochure with maps identifying the species of rhododendron. This is available at the Chamber of Commerce and other information distribution locations but *not* at the garden itself.

Much of the charm of the Rhododendron Garden is provided by its watery setting on a peninsula and an island in Crystal Springs Lake. A boardwalk crosses through the middle of the lake, providing a good place to feed the ducks and observe their behavior. Beds of water iris grow in the water at the edge of the pond. The garden is spectacular during the height of the blooming season from late April through mid-May, but it is also pleasant and less crowded at other times of year.

To proceed to Westmoreland Park from the Rhododendron Garden, walk south on SE 28th Ave. around Eastmoreland Golf Course to SE Bybee, which takes you on a bridge over the railroad tracks and SE McLoughlin Blvd. Turn left (S) off SE Bybee onto SE 22nd, which parallels the park.

WESTMORELAND PARK

Westmoreland Park is a strip almost a ½ mile long. Its most interesting features are the waterways—a sailboat pond, a well-populated duck pond, and a canal. You can follow the canal to the south end of the park. (The canal can also be followed north into the area of the retirement home.)

To follow Crystal Springs Creek from Westmoreland Park to its end at Johnson Creek Park requires walking several blocks on city streets. SE Nehalem St. forms the southern border of Westmoreland Park. Go west on SE Nehalem. Turn left (S) onto SE 21st, which will lead you to Johnson Creek Park.

JOHNSON CREEK PARK

This small gem is one of the prettiest Portland parks. You can walk out onto the grassy peninsula formed where clear Crystal Springs Creek joins muddy Johnson Creek. The contrast between the two streams is remarkable.

SAUVIE ISLAND

Walking Distance	Any distance; see hikes described below for specific suggestions.
Time to Spend	1 day or several
Setting	Sandy beach along the Columbia, pasture, oak groves, cottonwood and willow woods along lake shore.
Distance from Downtown Portland	About 11 miles to Sauvie Island Bridge
Driving Directions	N on Route 30 (NW St. Helen's Rd.) to Sauvie Island Bridge
Bus	Weekday commuting service from St. John's

IMPORTANT: The game management areas (which include all the nonprivate lands) are **closed** to the public, except for hunters, during the waterfowl season each year (approximately October 15-January 15).

NOTE: No drinking water or gasoline available on the island.

When you feel the need for space, come to this vast pastoral area close to Portland. Sauvie Island is very popular for a variety of recreational activities—boating, fishing, swimming, bird-watching, hunting, dog training, bike riding—but the island is so large that it never seems crowded once you get off the roads, and it is always possible to find a place to be alone with nature.

The Oregon State Game Commission has acquired more than 14,000 acres since 1947 with the purpose of preserving and developing the area for wintering waterfowl. Since the lands were purchased with fees collected from hunters, the Game Commission believes its policy of closing the area to nonhunters during the hunting season is justified. About half of the area is a perpetual game refuge, with the other half being open to hunting in season. Hunting of nongame species by permit occurs year round.

Sauvie Island contains a variety of valuable bird habitats— wetlands, pasture, oak woodlands, and patches of coniferous woodland. The best time for spotting birds is during the migratory seasons, particularly the fall migration from August through November. *A Checklist to the Birds of Sauvie Island* by Ronald J. Klein is available from the Portland Audubon Society.

In recent years the problem of smog has increased on Sauvie Island, which is often "socked in" when other areas are clear. You may want to scan the horizon before setting out for an excursion to the island.

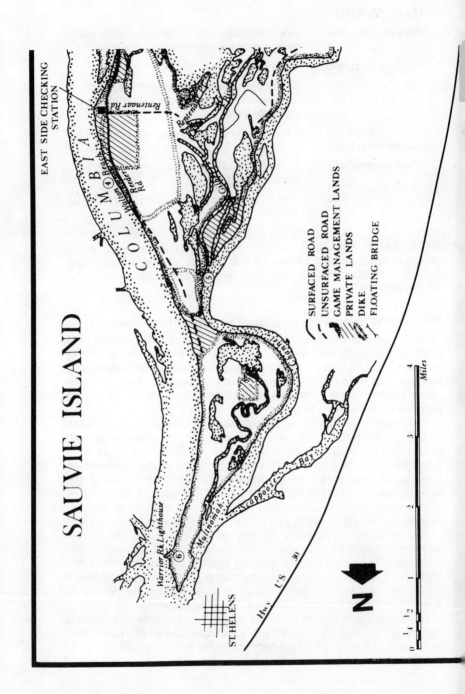

SAUVIE ISLAND

EAST SIDE CHECKING STATION

Rentenaar Rd

Beach

Wilton Reeder Rd

C O L U M B I A

Renten...

SURFACED ROAD
UNSURFACED ROAD
GAME MANAGEMENT LANDS
PRIVATE LANDS
DIKE
FLOATING BRIDGE

Channel

Bay

Multnomah.

Scappoose Bay

Warrior Rk Lighthouse

ST HELENS

Hwy US 30

N

0 ¼ ½ 1   2   3   4
                                  Miles

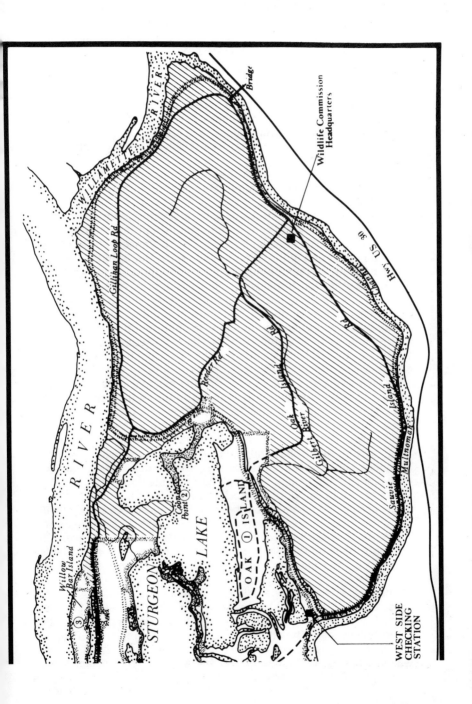

HISTORY

Sauvie Island was a major Indian population center. There may have been as many as 2000 living here in numerous villages of split cedar houses. They probably chose the area because food was plentiful—salmon, sturgeon, camas, and wapato. A tragic epidemic of "ague" (most likely malaria) from 1829-1835 completely wiped out the Indians.

Lewis and Clark camped on Sauvie Island. The Indians served them roast wapato, and the explorers bought a supply of the bulbs to augment their provisions.

The first permanent settlement was established by the Hudson's Bay Company. They had considered establishing their trading post on Sauvie Island but rejected it in favor of Ft. Vancouver because of the annual flooding and scarcity of beaver on the island. However, around 1838 they found a good use for the site as a dairy farm to produce butter for trade with the Russians in Alaska. Laurent Sauve, a French Canadian, was in charge of the Hudson's Bay dairy operation, which continued until the company was forced to withdraw in 1846 when the boundary line between the United States and Britain was set at the 49th parallel. Subsequently the island became open for homesteading under the Donation Land Law of 1850.

These early settlers led a very isolated existence. Families were widely separated because of the large size of the land claims (most were 640 acres) and because transportation was primarily by boat, since there were no roads. They had to endure the tribulation of annual spring flooding (and in some years, winter flooding as well). Most of the island was inundated during these floods, and the islanders had to keep close watch on the water level, ready to evacuate to the mainland with their cattle on steamboats.

In addition to dairying, livestock raising was an important activity here because the meadows on the island produced two crops of wild hay each year, before and after the spring flood. In later years the residents also earned some money selling ducks and geese to Portland meat markets and supplying feathers for feather beds. Because of its isolation, the island became a favorite location for bootleggers.

The ecology of Sauvie Island was changed radically by the construction of the dikes by the Army Corps of Engineers. Finished in 1941, they were one of the mammoth public works projects of the Depression years. The dikes brought an end to the annual flooding which had produced luxuriant meadows of wild grasses. Camas and wapato, abundant staples of the Indian diet, also disappeared.

These wild crops were replaced by cultivated legumes and grasses and vegetable crops. This is fertile farmland because the soil consists of topsoil which was washed down from the West Hills and deposited in annual layers before the dikes were built. (Fresh vegetables are sold at stands along the road, and some families make an annual pilgrimage to Sauvie Island to pick out Halloween pumpkins.) Much of the land in the Game Management Area, not enclosed by dikes (see map), is still close to its original condition. The level of the water here fluctuates with the level of the Columbia. The seclusion of Sauvie Island diminished gradually. Electricity came in 1936 and telephones in 1948. A county ferry was established in 1910, the road system was finished in 1941, and the bridge built in 1950. But even today, there is a rare tranquillity to be found on Sauvie Island.

Most of the information here came from an interesting little book, available at the Multnomah County Library: *The Story of Sauvies Island* by Omar C. Spencer (Binford & Mort, 1950). Mr. Spencer was a dairy farmer on the island.

If you are interested in the history of the island, be sure to pay a visit to the Bybee-Howell House. This 1856 homestead has been restored and furnished by the Oregon Historical Society. The house is open from June to October, and admission is free. The grounds are a good place to observe marsh birds during summer.

HIKES

The opportunities for hiking on Sauvie Island are practically unlimited. Much of the area is open because of cattle grazing, and you can just strike off cross-country and walk until you get to water, but you'd better take a map and compass (as well as drinking water) with you! We will describe some of our favorite hiking areas on the island for those who would like specific suggestions.

Oak Island

Directions: From the bridge turn off Sauvie Island Rd. onto Reeder Rd. Turn left off Reeder Rd. to Oak Island Rd. and follow it to the end.

Oak Island is really a peninsula which projects three miles into Sturgeon Lake, the largest of the multitude of lakes on Sauvie Island. Most of the island is covered with a grove of beautiful old Oregon white oaks.

Oak Island had special spiritual significance for the local Indians. Youths from the Indian village at Reeder Point on the Columbia would come for their fasting vigil, awaiting a revelation from their guardian spirit. There are also said to be two Indian dancing rings among the oaks, marked by bare ground where grass cannot grow.

Coon Point

Directions: From the bridge turn off Sauvie Island Rd. onto Reeder Rd. Stop at parking area by the dike. Climb to the top of the dike and head for the point, a distance of about 1½ miles.

This point jutting into Sturgeon Lake is a favorite fishing spot and a good place to see shore birds during migration.

Willow Bar Island

Directions: From the bridge turn off Sauvie Island Rd. onto Reeder Rd. Park in a big sandy area about ¾ mile beyond Marshall Beach Tavern sign. Traverse the sand dunes to get to the "island" (really another peninsula) about 2 miles long.

Here you can walk along old road beds through the willow woods or on the beach along the Columbia. It is interesting to come back to this area at different times of the year and note great changes in the water level.

Walton Beach

Directions: Take Sauvie Island Rd. to Reeder Rd. Parking area is ½ mile beyond the East Side Checking Station. Cross the dike to get to the beach.

Here open beach stretches for more than 2 miles along the Columbia. This is a favorite spot for retired fishermen.

Gilbert River

Directions: Sauvie Island Rd. to Reeder Rd. to turnoff for Gilbert Boat Ramp. Park in parking area at the boat ramp.

It is interesting to hike up the sliver of land between the Gilbert River and the chain of lakes. It is possible to cross to the other side of the lakes by means of the floating bridges at several points, but don't count on all the bridges being in place. The presence of these bridges keeps power boats out of the lakes. Rentenaar Pt. might be a good destination (about 3½ miles). The point offers a good view of the Sturgeon Lake area and could also be reached by a shorter hike from the end of Rentenaar Rd. Other hikes in the Gilbert River area are apparent from the map.

Warrior Rock

Directions: Sauvie Island Rd. to Reeder Rd. to the end.

Warrior Rock is a lava flow on the northern tip of Sauvie Island. The hike to the rock takes you about 3½ miles along the shore of the Columbia River. The rock was named by Lt. Broughton of the Vancouver expedition, who resolved a dispute with local Indians on the site. It was during his stay on Sauvie Island that Broughton named Mt. Hood.

The Game Commission recently purchased a piece of the neck of private land which had separated this peninsula from the rest of the public land on the island so that access is now possible to this wild area. Game Commission officials warned of Vietcong and Bigfoot in the vicinity, though the latter was reputed to be benign!

VANCOUVER HISTORICAL WALK

Walking Distance	2¾ miles one way
Time to Spend	½ day or more
Setting	Flat urban area
Distance from Downtown Portland	7¾ miles
Driving Directions	N on I-5 across the Interstate Bridge to Vancouver/Business exit. Turn L (W) onto 6th St. (where large sign reads Port, Main St.) Continue on 6th to Esther Short Park, the starting point for this walk.
Bus	From Portland, Tri-Met #5, Vancouver-Portland (does not run on Sunday)

Note: The inspiration for this walk and some of the information came from the ''Discovery Trail'' brochure published by the Vancouver Parks and Recreation Department. The Discovery Trail is an ambitious civic project with the goal of providing a 20-mile walkway which would encircle the City of Vancouver, linking its recreation and historic sites.

Vancouver, Washington, the oldest settlement in the Portland area, is a pleasant small town today, but in the mid-19th Century the Hudson's Bay Company outpost here was ''the economic, political, social and cultural hub of the Northwest.'' The museums along this walk can provide you with a wealth of historical information about the early days.

Sunday afternoon is the pleasantest time to take this walk because there is very little traffic downtown then. This flat route would also make a good bike ride at that time.

1. Esther Short Park

This green island in downtown is the original Vancouver Public Square, and there are several items of interest here.

1a. The **Slocum House** stands in the southwest corner of the park at 6th and Esther Streets. Built in 1867, this house, complete with widow's walk, exemplifies the ''Rhode Island architecture'' of Charles Slocum's Eastern childhood. It is now being put to good use as a community theater, the Old Slocum House Theatre Co.

Statues in the park portray appropriate historical models—the Pioneer Mothers' Statue and a hulking wooden statue of a dour Indian.

Railroad buffs and children will enjoy seeing the locomotive on display in the park.

2. St. James Catholic Church, 218 W. 12th St.

This does not look like an old building, but it was constructed in

1884 as the first masonry cathedral in Washington. It contains a hand-carved Belgian altar.

3. **Hidden House and Barn,** 100 W. 13th St.

This house, now a restaurant, was built in 1885 by Lowell Hidden, early civic leader and brickmaker. (He took up brickmaking at the urging of Mother Joseph, who needed a source of bricks for the construction of Providence Academy. See #5, Providence Academy.) More picturesque than the house is the barn behind it, currently being remodeled for offices.

4. **Clark County Historical Museum,** 16th and Main Sts.

This building, originally a Carnegie library, is now a museum containing many interesting exhibits, including life-size models of an 1890 country store, an 1873 print shop, and a 1900 doctor's office. The basement houses an extensive railroad exhibit. This free museum is open afternoons except Monday.

5. **Providence Academy,** 400 E. Evergreen Blvd.

This "House of Providence" was founded by Mother Joseph, a towering figure in early Washington history. This woman provides a wonderful model for modern feminists. Freed from traditional family responsibilities by holy orders, she had the opportunity to develop her talents in disparate fields. An outstanding administrator, she was also the first (non-Indian) artist and architect in the Northwest.

Mother Joseph was born in Quebec in 1823, joined the Sisters of Providence in Montreal in 1843, and came with four other sisters as missionaries to the Oregon country, arriving in Vancouver in 1856. By the early 1860s these indomitable women had established a whole complex of social service institutions: day and boarding schools, hospital, asylum, home for the aged, and orphanage.

To provide adequate housing for all these activities, Mother Joseph designed the Academy, drawing up the plans and superintending construction herself. Construction proceeded piece-meal over the years, as funds became available. (The sisters helped to finance their activities by begging trips to mining camps. In addition to the other hazards of wilderness travel, these journeys were enlivened by encounters with robbers and Indians.)

The school opened in 1874, and the entire structure was finished in 1892. Of particular interest is the chapel (on the second floor) with graceful three-story arches and "Carpenter gothic" details on the woodwork. Mother Joseph made some of the statues, benches, and the five carved altars in her basement workshop. Other notable features are the cupola and bell-tower, which offer a fine view of the confluence of the Willamette and Columbia Rivers. The heart-shaped drive in front of the building is also unusual.

In the 20th Century, many of the Academy's functions were taken over by other agencies, although the school boomed during World

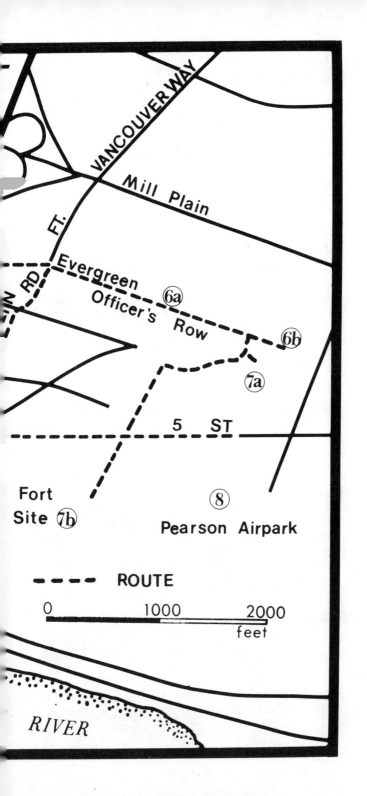

VANCOUVER WAY

Mill Plain

FT.

Evergreen

RD

Officer's Row

⑥a

⑥b

⑦a

5 ST

Fort
Site ⑦b

⑧

Pearson Airpark

▬ ▬ ▬ ▬ ROUTE

0   1000   2000
                              feet

RIVER

War II when Vancouver was crowded with war workers and their families. The school closed in 1966 and was then vacant for several years. Threatened with demolition, it was rescued by Robert Hidden, Lowell Hidden's grandson, who purchased it in 1969.

Today life has returned to the imposing old structure, with specialty shops and offices occupying many of the old classrooms. An excellent natural foods restaurant is among the tenants, making this a good lunch stop. (The shops are closed on Sundays.) In contrast to many other recycled buildings, modernization has not damaged the appeal of this charming building.

(Much of this information came from "A Brief Historical Sketch of the Academy," an attractive and informative booklet on sale at the Academy.)

6. Officers' Row

It is very pleasant to stroll along this tree-lined street between the charming white frame houses with their prominent porches and columns on one side of the street and the sweeping lawns dotted with firs on the other. There are nice views of the Columbia River to the south.

These substantial houses were constructed between 1849 and 1906 as homes for the officers of the U.S. Army post established at Vancouver after it became American territory.

6a. The **U.S. Grant Museum** at 1106 E. Evergreen Blvd. is the oldest house on Officers' Row. It was a log structure later covered with siding. The building served as post headquarters for many years and is named for the illustrious tenant who had an office here while a quartermaster in 1852-53. The museum is open afternoons except Thursday.

6b. The **Marshall House** at 1310 E. Evergreen Blvd. is distinguished from its neighbors by a jaunty tower. This house was built in 1886 as a residence for the commanding officer. It is named for George C. Marshall, who lived in it from 1936-39, later going on to become an important general during World War II, Secretary of State, and architect of the Marshall Plan for European recovery after the war. The building is now local headquarters for the Red Cross, Campfire Girls, Girl Scouts, and United Way.

7. Fort Vancouver National Historic Site

If you haven't been here before, this stop will probably be the highpoint of your walk. There is much information here, agreeably presented.

7a. The **Visitor Center** has displays depicting the central role of this Hudson's Bay Company station in the early history of the area.

7b. The **reconstructed fort,** a quarter of a mile down the hill from the Visitor Center, is a facsimile of the original stockade and several of the buildings inside it. During the summer "living history" exhibits are presented here, with Park Service employees enacting the roles of the inhabitants of Fort Vancouver.

Also on the grounds of the National Historic Site are a picnic area adjacent to the Visitor Center and a children's playground down the hill.

8. Pearson Airpark

This airport has had a varied history. Originally a cultivated field of the Hudson's Bay Co., next a pasture, then an Army airfield, the site is now a municipal airport. The airport was a division point for the first air mail service in 1926. Pearson Airpark is most famous as the 1937 landing site of three Soviet aviators pioneering the transpolar route. They embarked from Moscow in an At-25 monoplane and were enroute to San Francisco when shortage of fuel forced them to land here.

It's fun to survey the small planes parked in the parking lot (just like cars!) along E. 5th Street.

Note: To return to your starting point, you must walk back up to Evergreen Blvd. to cross over I-5 (see map).

VANCOUVER FITNESS LOOP

Walking or Jogging Distance	2-mile loop
Time to Spend	Depends on your pace!
Setting	Section 1, large flat grassy field studded with Douglas firs Section 2, flat brushy area
Distance from Downtown Portland	8¾ miles
Driving Directions	N on I-5 to Mill Plain Blvd. exit in Vancouver; E on Mill Plain to Fort Vancouver Way; N (R) on Ft. Vancouver Way to junction with McLoughlin Blvd.
Bus	From Portland take Tri-Met #5, Vancouver-Portland, to Vancouver (does not run on Sunday). Then you can walk about ¾ mile or take Vancouver Transit #3 Rosemere (does not run on Sunday).

The Fitness Loop is part of the Discovery Trail, a proposed 20-mile pedestrian path around Vancouver. (See Vancouver Historical Walk for more information.) This part was completed through the efforts of the Alki Junior Women's Club which coordinated the project, raising funds and securing the cooperation of the various governmental agencies involved. The loop was "specifically designed to challenge the physical abilities of each individual."

In Section 1 the path goes through the grass and along an old dirt road. For stops 8, 9, 10, and 11, be sure to go to the *end* of the field along the fence (don't turn off on the road that comes first).

Section 2 is more interesting, consisting of a thicket of deciduous bushes attractive to birds. The land here was donated by the federal government for a Central Park "to be retained primarily in a natural state." There is a cross trail penetrating the brush between Stations 14 and 18. On a mound near Station 18, you can view a luxuriant display of poison hemlock (identified by the red spots on the stem).

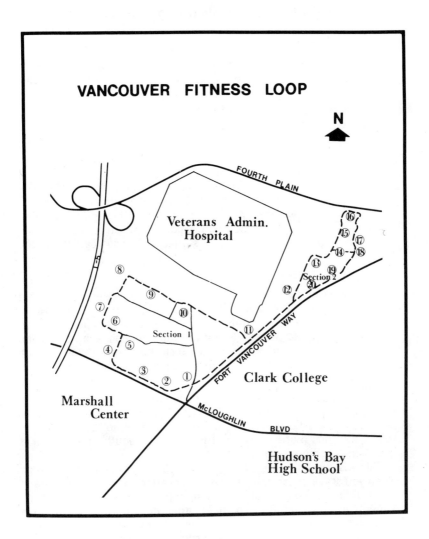

VANCOUVER FITNESS LOOP

N

FOURTH PLAIN

Veterans Admin. Hospital

16
15
17
14
18
13
19
Section 2
12
20

8
9
7
10
6
Section 1
11
4 5
FORT VANCOUVER WAY
3 2 1
Clark College

Marshall Center

McLOUGHLIN BLVD

Hudson's Bay High School

RIDGEFIELD NATIONAL WILDLIFE REFUGE

Walking Distance Carty Unit, up to 7 miles
River S and Roth Units, 8 miles or more

Time to Spend ½ to 1 day

Setting Flood plain and dikes; knolls, small lakes and still rivers; oak, cottonwood and willow woods.

Distance from Downtown Portland 25 miles

Driving Directions N I-5 to Ridgefield, Washington exit. Proceed W on exit road (Washington 501) to Ridgefield.
for **River S and Roth Units,** turn L (S) on S. 9th St. and then R (W) onto entrance road.
For **Carty Unit** proceed through the town of Ridgefield, following the street as it turns R (N). The signed entrance road is up the hill.

Bus No service

Season of Use: IMPORTANT: The refuge management asks that hikers **not** visit the south units (River S and Roth) when hunting is going on. Hunting is permitted on Saturdays, Sundays, and Wednesdays during the Washington State duck hunting season, which runs from approximately October 15 through January 15 each year.

As indicated on the map, the refuge is separated into two parts by Lake River. The north unit, Carty, is probably best for hiking because it is closed to hunting all year round, is not penetrated by roads, and has more interesting terrain. The south units, River S and Roth, are more open.

This vast wildlife refuge of more than 3000 acres is the place to go when you crave unconfined space and isolation. Here you are free to roam widely without constantly bumping into fences or boundaries. Though you are unlikely to meet other people here, even on a weekend, you probably will meet cows, so watch your step! Because the cows keep the grass short, you can walk almost anywhere. Cow paths and dikes provide convenient "trails."

There is only one short designated hiking trail, the Oak Grove Trail, a self-guiding nature trail in the Carty Unit. Meandering beside marshes, over streams, and through woods, this ½-mile loop trail guides you through groves of massive Oregon white oak. (Brochures for the trail are available only at the refuge office at 3rd and Mill St. in the town of Ridgefield.)

Because of the vastness of the refuge, the lack of an organized trail system, and the presence of many similar-looking lakes in the Carty Unit, it is easy to get lost here. If you are going very far into the refuge, take a map and compass. In fact, this would be a good place to practice orienteering!

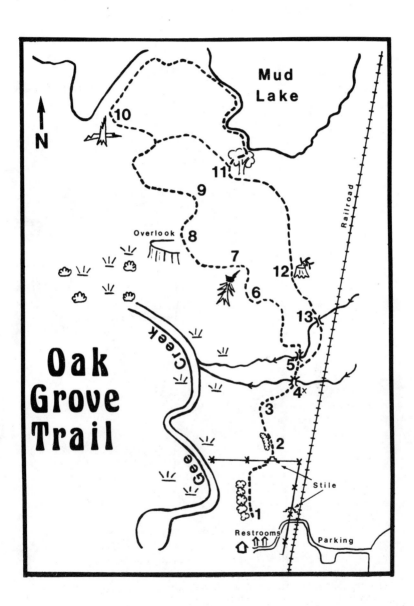

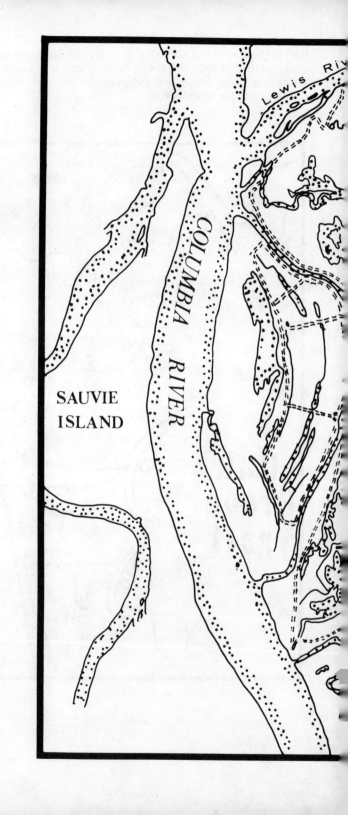

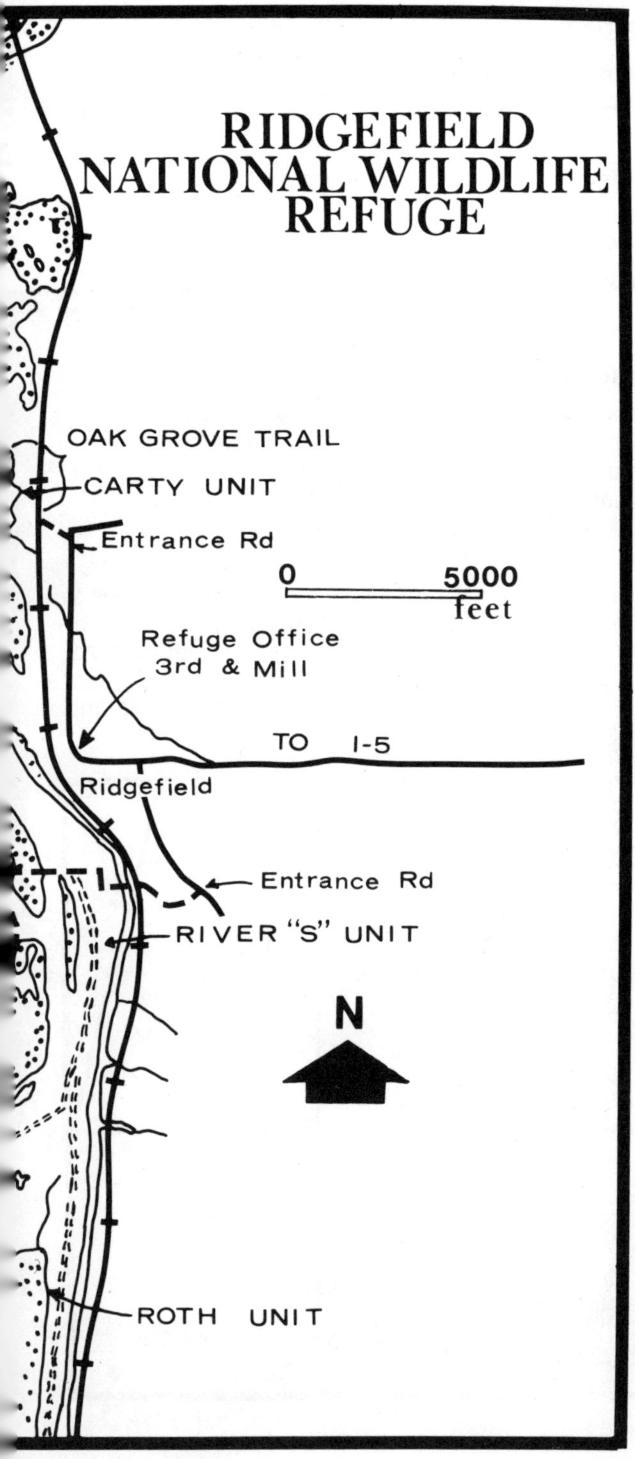

RIDGEFIELD NATIONAL WILDLIFE REFUGE

OAK GROVE TRAIL

CARTY UNIT

Entrance Rd

0   5000
feet

Refuge Office
3rd & Mill

TO I-5

Ridgefield

Entrance Rd

RIVER "S" UNIT

N

ROTH UNIT

WHIPPLE CREEK PARK

Walking Distance	3-4 miles round trip
Time to Spend	1½-2 hours; allow more time in case you get lost!
Setting	Dense forest of mature conifers
Distance from Downtown Portland	20 miles
Driving Directions	N on I-5 into Washington to Battleground, 179th St. exit. W on 179th St. to NW 31st Ave. S (L) on 31st. to dead end.
Bus	No bus service

This little-known and little-used natural site will be especially appreciated by residents of the Vancouver area. Completely undeveloped and unmarked, it is not really a "park" yet. The dark, mossy rainforest has a primeval quality.

TRAILS

A network of horse use trails penetrates the forest on both sides of Whipple Creek. There is a large area of trails but few exits or entrances, so that it may be difficult to find your way out. (In fact this was the only place we got lost while doing the field work for this book.) You should also be forewarned that the trails are steep and very muddy in places.

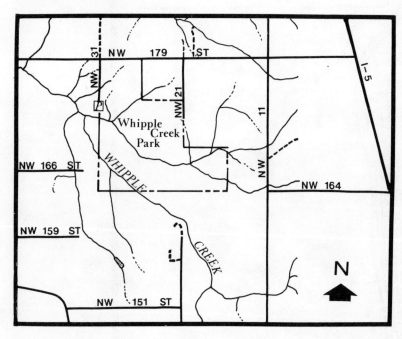

DAVID DOUGLAS PARK

Walking Distance	½ to 1 mile
Time to Spend	1 hour
Setting	Wooded canyon
Distance from Downtown Portland	Enjoy this park if you're in the area; but don't drive from Portland.
Driving Directions	From Vancouver, drive E on Mill Plain Blvd. to N Garrison Rd.; turn L (N) on Garrison to the park entrance road. (Trails also start off of NE Andreson Rd.)
Bus	Vancouver Transit #4/4A Fourth Plain and #5/5A Heights North/South (do not run on Sunday)

This small canyon provides Vancouver residents with a nice walk in pretty woods.

There is a network of trails down the bluff and through the ravine at the west side of the park. Many trails are very steep, but if you keep looking, it is possible to find a gentle descent. It is easy to get momentarily lost in the maze of trails, but it is such a small park that there is no reason to worry!

WASHOUGAL BEACH

Walking Distance	Dike, 8 miles round trip Beach, 1½ miles round trip (dependent on water level)
Time to Spend	½ - 1 day
Setting	Sandy beach; dike road through pasture land near the Columbia shore; sweeping views
Distance from Downtown Portland	25 miles
Driving Directions	N on I-5 across the Interstate Bridge to Camas exit, a sudden right just after the bridge. Continue on this road (Washington 14) beyond Camas and most of Washougal to 32nd St. Turn R (S) on 32nd, and drive through the industrial area to a parking area at the end of the street by the dike.
Bus	Greyhound or Evergreen Stage

This trip provides easy access from Portland to a fine sandy beach. Here are wide vistas of the Columbia River and Gorge from the less frequented north shore. When the water is warm enough, swimming is excellent. The short trail to the beach takes off from the other side of the dike. The distance you can walk along the beach varies with the water level (which is affected by tides as well as the volume of water in the river), but you can usually walk at least ½ mile in either direction.

The dike provides a long walk from a higher vantage point. (With a surface of packed gravel, it is also very good for bike riding.) In addition to views of the river and mountains, there are charming pastoral vistas closer at hand. There is access to the beach from several points along the dike, depending upon the water level. (At low water you could probably walk and wade from a point near Ft. Vancouver across to Reed Island. If you try this, beware of tide changes.)

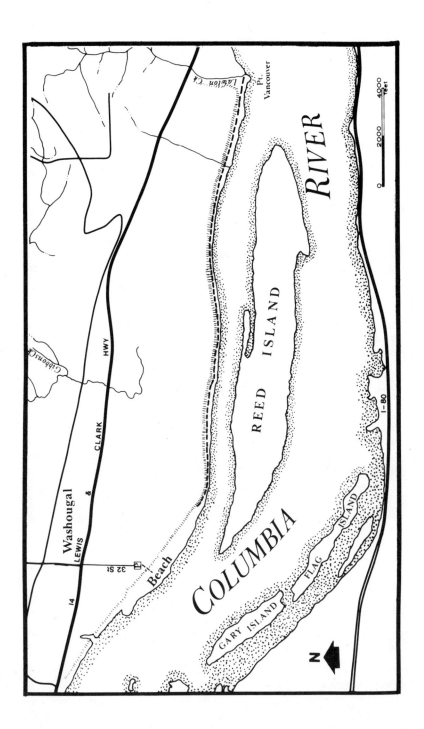

BATTLEGROUND LAKE STATE PARK

Walking Distance	1 mile around the lake
Time to Spend	1½ to 2 hours
Setting	Wooded lakeshore
Distance from Downtown Portland	28 miles
Driving Directions	N on I-5 to Battleground exit in Washington. Follow 502 to Battleground. Follow signs for "State Park," turning off 502 on NE Heisson Rd.
Bus	No service

Battleground Lake has been called "a jewel among the foothills of the Cascades," and it is indeed an exquisite mountain lake. It occupies the small but deep crater of an extinct volcano. Mature conifers grow up to the waterline, and the state park management has left almost all the shoreline uncleared, except for the trail itself.

Facilities of the state park include a small gravel swimming beach, picnic tables, campsites, and an imaginative playground made of natural wood, ropes, and tires. (It is too bad that overnight camping is permitted here, as the increased wear may damage this small gem of a park.)

TRAILS

A trail through the deep woods encircles the lake. This signed trail starts at the north end of the parking lot. (A gravel trail on the upper level goes to walk-in campsites.) Because the trail is almost completely in shade, a hot summer day is a good time to come here, except for the fact that it may be crowded then.

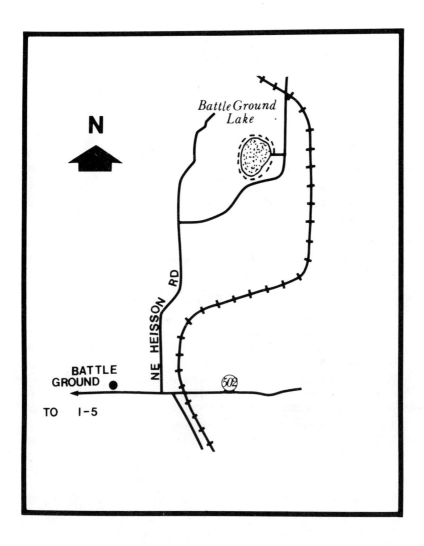

N

Battle Ground Lake

NE HEISSON RD

BATTLE
GROUND ●

TO   I-5

502

LACAMAS PARK - ROUND LAKE

Walking Distance	3 miles, if all trails are walked
Time to Spend	1½ hours, more if you want to swim and picnic
Setting	Wooded lake shore and gorge
Distance from Downtown Portland	25 miles
Driving Directions	N on I-5 across the Interstate bridge to Camas exit, a sudden R just after the bridge. Continue on this road (Washington 14) to the exit for Lacamas Lake Park. Go N through Camas on Washington 500 to the park.
Bus	No good service (Evergreen Stage goes to downtown Camas about 1½ miles from the park.)

Lacamas Park lies along the shore of Round Lake, the man-made lower arm of Lacamas Lake. This county park is considered "undeveloped," and future development is planned. We hope this will not degrade the natural area. Swimming is good here, and in appropriate weather you can expect crowds. Watch out for poison oak.

TRAILS

To get to all three trails, walk through the pretty wooded picnic area along the lake shore to the south end of the lake. From here there are trails downstream along both sides of Lacamas Creek, which is enclosed in a steep gorge created by sandstone outcrops.

1. The trail down the west side takes off just before the dam over the main lake, goes along beside a pond, across a dam, and on through the woods, ending at a school on the outskirts of Camas.

2. For the trail which goes down the east side of the creek and the trail which continues farther around the lake, cross the cement dam at the end of the lake. The east side creek trail ends at an open grassy bluff. A sandstone outcrop makes a series of small falls in the gorge here.

3. Another trail continues around the lake, then goes up the hill ending at an open rocky viewpoint.

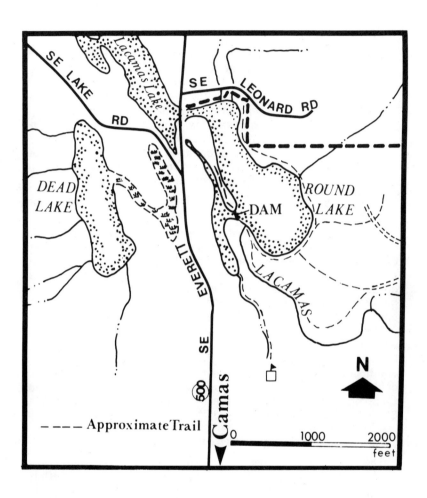

SE LAKE

RD

SE LEONARD RD

Lacamas Lake

DEAD
LAKE

DAM

ROUND
LAKE

LACAMAS

SE

500

Camas

SE EVERETT

N

- - - Approximate Trail

0   1000   2000
                         feet

BURNT BRIDGE CREEK GREENWAY

Walking Distance	2½ miles round trip
Time to Spend	2 hours
Setting	Marsh, brush, conifer woods
Distance from Downtown Portland	13 miles
Driving Directions	N on I-5 into Washington to 78th St. exit; W on 78th to Fruit Valley Rd.; L (S) on Fruit Valley Rd. to NW Bernie Dr.; L off Fruit Valley Rd. onto NW Bernie Dr. The entrance (opposite the "Speed 25" sign) is marked by a brown sign indicating "Wildlife and Natural Area." Parking is prohibited along NW Bernie Dr. here, but there is room for two cars to park off the road in front of the sign.
Bus	Vancouver Transit #2, Capitol Hill, goes near (does not run on Sunday).

Burnt Bridge Creek Greenway is an especially nice discovery for residents of Vancouver, Washington. There are three different ecological zones here on three different levels: a marshy area next to the creek and slough; a brushy area higher up where the main trail goes; and conifer woods on the top level. This diverse wildlife habitat was saved from inclusion in the adjacent housing development by the efforts of the Nature Conservancy.

The League of Women Voters in Clark County is also concerned about the quality of Burnt Bridge Creek in its 8-mile course through Clark County. The water is badly polluted by septic tank overflow, and flooding and erosion have been caused by paving over of much of the land that used to soak up the rainfall. To join the Action Campaign to restore the creek, contact the League at 604 W. 32nd St. in Vancouver (695-0553).

TRAILS

The main use trail goes above the slough formed where Burnt Bridge Creek joins Vancouver Lake and upstream along Burnt Bridge Creek. Other use trails go down from the new housing development through the conifer level to the main trail. To appreciate what has been saved, you can make a loop trip back to your car through the subdivision by going up one of the conifer trails to NW Bernie Drive.

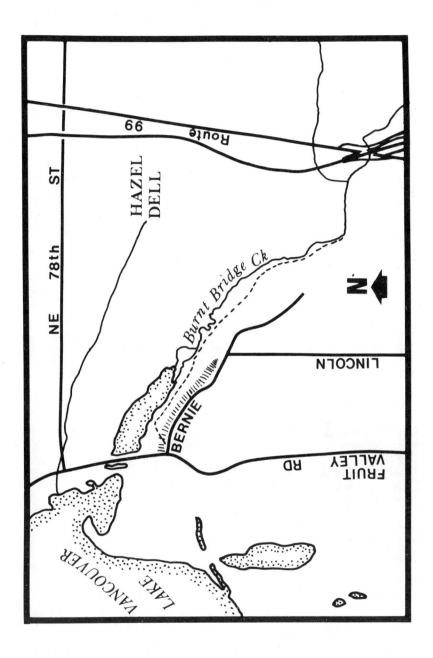

LEE FALLS & HAINES FALLS

Walking Distance 5 miles round trip from Lee Falls to Haines Falls; 5 additional miles round trip to Lee Falls if road is not passable (see below).

Setting Dirt road along wooded stream

Distance from Downtown Portland 30 miles

Driving Directions U.S. 26 to Forest Grove turnoff or Oregon 8 to Forest Grove. Then S on Oregon 47 about 4½ miles to Cherry Grove turnoff. In Cherry Grove follow the main road around the south side of town. Turn left onto a small dirt road at the Nixon mailbox, about the point where the pavement ends on the main road. (The turnoff to the falls is unmarked and difficult to find, so you may want to ask in Cherry Grove for directions.)

Lee Falls is about 2½ miles down this **deeply rutted** dirt road. In wet times there are **many puddles** to cross. The road was passable for an average car in May 1977 but does not seem to be maintained so may become worse. If the road is not passable for your car, the road itself makes a pleasant walk with frequent turnoffs by the stream.

Bus No bus service.

It is hard to believe that the clean, fast-moving stream here is the Tualatin River, far upstream from where we normally see it. Lee Falls is about 70 feet wide with a 20-foot drop. There is a nice pool under the falls for swimming in hot weather, and you can wade across the stream above the falls and then follow use trails up the other shore.

The road is blocked by a gate at Lee Falls, but you can walk 2½ miles further upstream to Haines Falls.

The whole area is not maintained, and unfortunately garbage abounds. Watch out for poison oak.

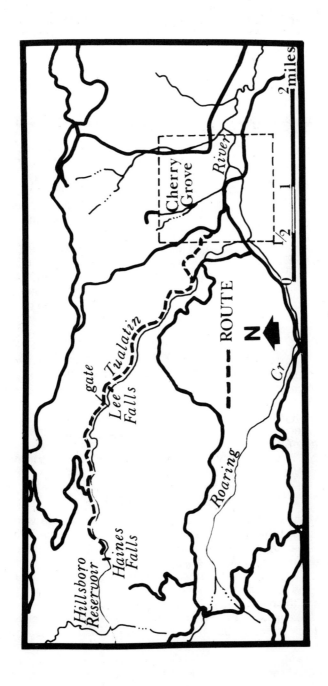

ST. MARY'S FOREST AND JENKINS ROAD FOREST

Walking Distance	**St. Mary's Forest,** 1-1½ miles round trip **Jenkins Road Forest,** 1 mile round trip
Time to Spend	**St. Mary's Forest,** 1½-2 hours **Jenkins Road Forest,** 1 hour
Setting	Oak and fir woods; St. Mary's Forest also has a marsh, creeks, and a pond
Driving Directions	W from Beaverton on Oregon 8 (Tualatin Valley Highway) **St. Mary's Forest:** Go past St. Mary's Boys' Home and Our Lady of Peace Retreat Center on TV Highway. Turn R (N) onto SW 170th Ave. Park along the side of the road wherever you can. The best entrance trail starts near the ''Speed 40'' sign. **Jenkins Road Forest:** Turn R (N(off TV Highway at SW 145th Ave. (Murray Rd.). Turn L (W) on Jenkins Rd. A good entrance is at the SW corner of this intersection or along the S side of Jenkins Rd.
Bus	#57, Forest Grove/Hillsboro/Beaverton, goes along TV Highway.

These neighboring tracts of land are well worth exploration by residents of Beaverton and Aloha. Though heavily disturbed, they are quite wild in comparison to their residential and industrial surroundings. These areas have been identified by the Nature Conservancy as valuable natural islands within metropolitan Washington County, and we hope they can be reserved for public use. This is particularly important in view of the dearth of large parks in Washington County.

ST. MARY'S FOREST

St. Mary's Forest is composed of 400 acres of dense woods and open fields at the confluence of Cedar Mill and Beaverton Creeks.

This little-known tract of land, with its diversity of vegetation and aquatic habitats, is a state game refuge (while it lasts). Beaver, wood ducks, and great horned owls live here. Plants of interest include the rare giant trillium, nightshade growing along the creek, cattails in the pond, and poison oak bushes.

The area lacks a rational system of trails, so the walker must bushwhack or follow use trails taking off from 170th south of the stream. For the intrepid, an interesting overgrown trail starts north of the stream.

The St. Mary's Forest property is currently for sale, and the

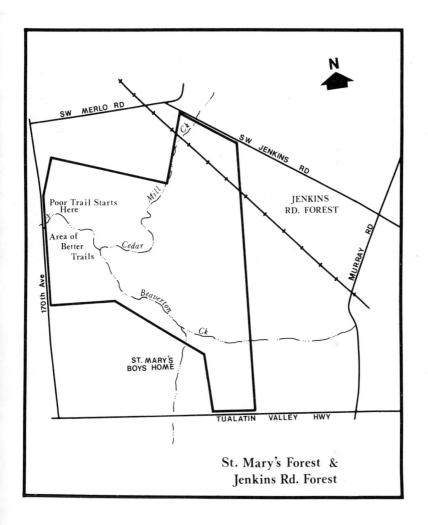

N

SW MERLO RD

SW JENKINS RD

Ck

JENKINS
RD. FOREST

MURRAY RD

Mill

Poor Trail Starts
Here

Area of
Better
Trails

Cedar

170th Ave

Beaverton

Ck

ST. MARY'S
BOYS HOME

TUALATIN VALLEY HWY

St. Mary's Forest &
Jenkins Rd. Forest

Oregon State Parks Branch would like to purchase it for a Regional Conservation Area. A suggested development plan includes a visitor center, bridge, trails, and wildlife blinds. The realization of this plan depends on appropriation of the necessary funds by the 1979 legislature. A citizens' group from the Beaverton area, Friends of St. Mary's Forest State Park, is actively promoting this park proposal.

JENKINS ROAD FOREST

Jenkins Road Forest is located less than a mile outside the city limits of Beaverton across the railroad tracks and northeast of St. Mary's Forest. Although partially logged in the past, this 100-acre woods is still a good example of successional oak and fir forest in the Willamette Valley. It is a surprise to come across scattered tall ponderosa pines. This woods is also a state game refuge, and animal life is said to include deer, raccoon, opossum, owl, quail, and other birds.

Old roadbeds are the best trails. Unfortunately parts of the area have been used as a garbage dump.

SCOGGINS VALLEY PARK - HENRY HAGG RESERVOIR

Walking Distance	10½ miles when trail system is completed 3-5 miles currently
Time to Spend	½ to 1 day
Setting	Lake shore, grassy and wooded
Distance from Downtown Portland	30 miles (7 miles SW of Forest Grove)
Driving Directions	U.S. 26 to Forest Grove turnoff **or** Oregon 8 to Forest Grove. Then S on Oregon 47 to park turnoff.
Bus	No bus service.
Parking Fee	$1.00

Henry Hagg Lake is a typical reservoir, popular for motorized water sports. It still has a bare look, which will probably disappear once natural vegetation has a chance to return to the shore. A road encircles the entire lake, and long-range plans call for a 10½-mile hiking trail between the road and the lake.

The project was built by the U.S. Bureau of Reclamation, which operates the dam. The park is now administered by Washington County, and a $1.00 parking fee is charged to help recoup expenses.

Until this park was created, Washington County lacked any major public park. To meet this recreation need (as well as other public needs described below) three reservoirs were planned. However, Henry Hagg is the only one which has been financed and built. To the relief of environmentalists, plans for Rock Creek Reservoir and McKay Creek Reservoir have apparently been shelved.

Despite the huge volume of water that flows through the Tualatin River during spring runoff, Washington County suffers from drought during the dry summer months. Therefore the water impounded behind Scoggins Dam will serve to augment municipal water supplies and irrigate farm land. Regulation of flow in the Tualatin River should prevent floods during the rainy season while ameliorating pollution during the summer when the normal flow is very low. Water quality is expected to improve enough to maintain a run of silver salmon.

The price paid for these benefits, in addition to the financial cost, was the destruction of a beautiful natural valley. Phase II of the Tualatin Project calls for the flooding and damming of the adjacent Patton Valley, and if you have an opinion about this, now is the time to speak out.

Though it is recognized that construction of the dam and reservoir reduced available wildlife habitat, management efforts have been made to maintain wildlife populations. Black-tailed deer and elk winter in several areas around the lake. Red-tailed hawks live here, and dead trees were left standing at the upper end of the reservoir

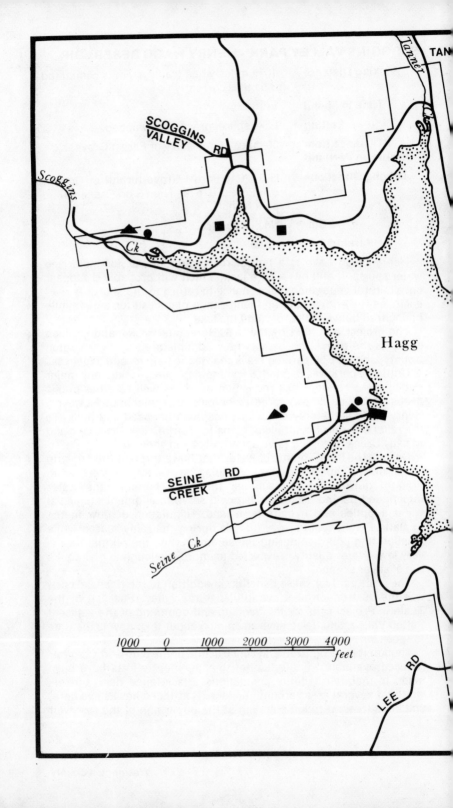

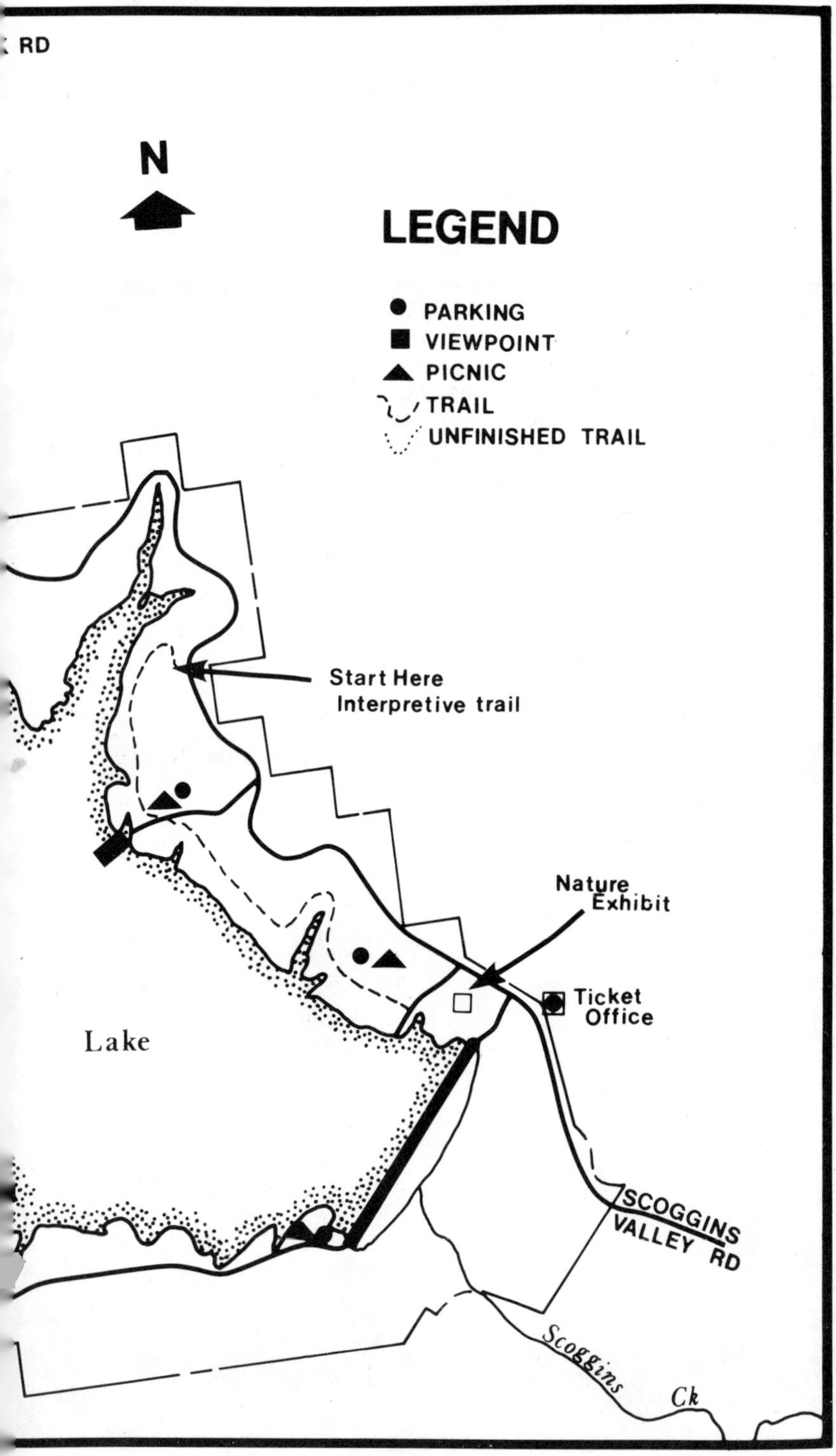

RD

N

LEGEND

● PARKING
■ VIEWPOINT
▲ PICNIC
⌒⌣ TRAIL
⋯ UNFINISHED TRAIL

Start Here
Interpretive trail

Nature
Exhibit

Ticket
Office

Lake

SCOGGINS
VALLEY RD

Scoggins Ck

in the hope of attracting ospreys and possibly bald eagles. We saw a beaver while we were there. Botanists are excited about a rare species of orchid which grows in the park.

It is best to come to Scoggins Valley Park in winter or spring when the reservoir is full. It is unattractive in late summer and fall when the water line has receded.

TRAILS

CETA and YCC crews work at trail-building every summer. The best section of trail completed so far is the interpretive trail which winds for 1½ to 2 miles through a wooded area above the lake. A trail guide is being prepared by the Washington County IED. An informative nature display has been set up at the end of the interpretive trail (see map). For the most up-to-date information about other sections of the trail, inquire at the ticket booth at the park entrance. In addition to trails, grassy areas along the shore are good for roaming cross-country.

GEORGE ROGERS PARK

Walking Distance	3 miles or less
Time to Spend	2-3 hours
Setting	Manicured formal garden; sandy and rocky riverfront; trail up wild deep canyon; old road along bluff facing the river
Distance from Downtown Portland	8 miles
Driving Directions	Oregon 43 (SW Macadam Ave.) to Lake Oswego. No sign marks the entrance to the park. Turn left at the ball field at the south end of Main St. just past the A & W. Park opposite the ball field. (You can drive down to a parking area closer to the river, but it is nicer to walk down the hill to better enjoy the vista of the river.)
Bus	#36, Oregon City-South Shore

HISTORICAL BACKGROUND

The area encompassed by George Rogers Park, today a prime recreation site, was in the past an important industrial center. The settlement of the area began when Albert Alonzo Durham, who came west from New York State, built a sawmill on the creek in 1850, and named the place Oswego after Oswego, New York. Other settlers followed, and the town developed here. Iron ore deposits were found in the nearby hills, and early promoters prophesied that the town would become the "Pittsburgh of the West." In the 1880s more than 300 men lived and worked at the site. (The area where the ball field is now was a Chinatown.)

Today there are only two visible remains of all this activity: the iron furnace enshrined in a corner of the oval garden, and the little cement building at the back of the canyon where the first electric power was generated for the town. An historical inscription at the furnace explains more about the iron industry.

The park was named for George Rogers, an immigrant from Madeira and early grocer in the area, who worked hard to make the park a reality.

If you are interested in the history of the Lake Oswego area, an interesting document to peruse is *In Their Own Words: A Collection of Reminiscences of Early Oswego, Oregon,* edited by volunteers and staff of the Lake Oswego Public Library.

WALKS

The waterfront section of the park with its "beach" (half sand, half mud) is a busy scene on warm weekends—small boys playing with inner tubes, power boats loading and unloading, sunbathers. A steamboat landing was here in early days, and the area at the mouth

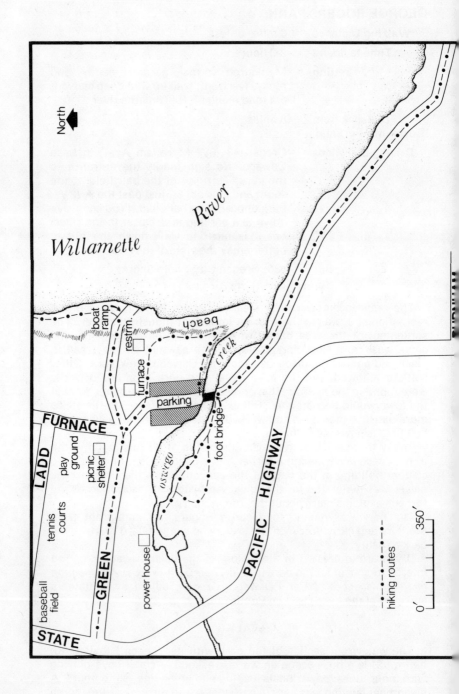

North

Willamette

River

boat ramp

restrm.

beach

creek

furnace

parking

foot bridge

FURNACE

LADD

play ground

picnic shelter

GREEN

tennis courts

oswego

PACIFIC HIGHWAY

baseball field

power house

STATE

hiking routes

0'   350'

of the creek was a popular spring campsite for gypsies. From the beach you can walk a ways upstream along the river over rocks or along a path through grass till you get to a private property sign. Oswego Creek was called Sucker Creek by the early settlers and Waluga Creek (Wild Swan Creek) by the Indians. To reach the trail along the creek from the parking lot, walk across the foot bridge and turn right. This is a lush canyon with mossy rocks and licorice ferns, and the creek is ideal for wading—a perfect spot for a hot day. (On a chilly day the open area of the park facing the Willamette is more attractive.) The trail becomes more and more inviting as it goes deeper into the canyon, ending abruptly in an area of large boulders. From here the adventurous can scramble on and find a truly private nook. The canyon would seem very secluded if it weren't for traffic noise.

There is an old road along the wooded riverbank south of the canyon which has been publicized as a bike trail (and it is a good one), so watch out for bike riders on busy weekends. In winter this road provides clear vistas of the Willamette. The road ends at a footbridge across another verdant canyon at Old River Rd. For a longer walk you can continue south along Old River Rd., which is peaceful and little traveled. There are occasional spots where you can get down to the river (but watch out for poison oak). This is a nice walk for a mile south to the West Linn boundary where you reach a developed area of houses between the road and the river.

MARY YOUNG STATE PARK &
CEDAR ISLAND

Walking Distance	Waterfront including Cedar Island, 2 miles round trip Perimeter trail, 1½ miles loop
Time to Spend	½ to 1 day
Setting	Second growth forest; open fields; open and brushy shore (some wading may be necessary)
Distance from Downtown Portland	10 miles
Driving Directions	S on Oregon 43 (SW Macadam Ave. in Portland) through Lake Oswego and beyond Marylhurst College to Mary Young State Park on the outskirts of West Linn.
Bus	#36, Oregon City-South Shore

The land for this new state park was donated by Mary S. and Thomas E. Young with the stipulation that the "property shall be kept and maintained as nearly as possible in its natural condition." Though it is fairly small, jammed between housing developments in an urban area, Mary Young State Park has a good deal to offer the walker who craves natural surroundings, and if all options are pursued, quite a long walk can be had. The picnic tables are attractively sited in private nooks in the woods.

WATERFRONT WALK

Up to 2 miles in dry years. (Avoid this area on Sunday afternoons when the tranquillity is disturbed by power boats.)

Trails descend through the woods to the river from several points in the picnic area. When the water level isn't too high, you can walk 1000 feet *south* along the river before coming to private homes. The way goes along a grassy path, then through a rocky area, past a miniature sandy beach, past more rocks, to a triangular orange Coast Guard marker labeled "20." (In years of normal water, you may be wading part way.)

Walking *north* along the waterfront, you traverse a field of cut grass with side trails over to the river's edge. A little farther on, the grass is no longer cut, but you can bushwhack or follow use trails, if you don't mind climbing over fallen trees, etc. You are now in Cedar Island County Park.

You may get your feet wet crossing over to Cedar Island; it's best to wear tennis shoes for this walk. The island is a high open area covered with cottonwood and Scotch broom (not a trace of a cedar tree!). For easy walking on the island, follow the dirt road out to its end opposite the boat-launching site.

Cedar Island provides excellent views up and down the Willamette and is a wonderful spot for bird watching.

PERIMETER TRAIL. 1½ miles

As its name implies, the Perimeter Trail circles around the borders of the park. You can join up with it at either the far north or far south corners of the parking lot, where signs indicate the trail.

The north part of this trail is our favorite. Here a wooden plank walkway descends to the waterfront through a particularly lush canyon. In the other direction (west, away from the river) the trail winds around and up and down through several small canyons, passes a couple of gigantic old-growth Douglas firs, and altogether gives the feeling of being far from civilization.

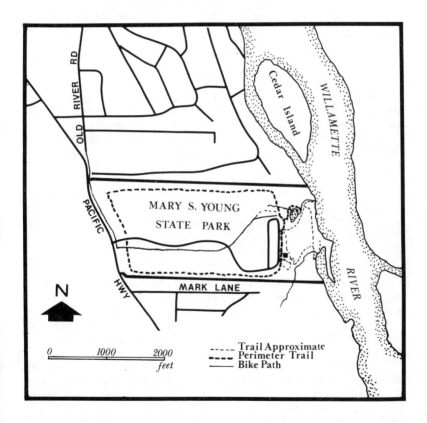

OSWEGO CANAL

Walking Distance	2 miles round trip
Time to Spend	2-3 hours
Setting	Quiet dirt road; wooded path along canal; fields
Distance from Downtown Portland	12 miles
Driving Directions	S on Oregon 43 (SW Macadam Ave. in Portland) to Lake Oswego. Turn R onto McVey Ave. at the road junction at the south end of town. McVey Ave. becomes Market Rd. Turn R off Market Rd. onto Childs Rd. about two miles from the junction. Turn R off Childs Rd. onto Canal Rd. at the blue sign reading "Park closes at 10 P.M., etc." Park at the side of the road.
Bus	No good service

HISTORY

The Oswego Canal was part of a grand scheme of the 1870s to provide transportation by water between Portland and the Tualatin Valley. Steamboats would proceed up the Willamette to Sucker Creek (Oswego Creek today) where they would progress up to Lake Oswego through a series of locks, then through the canal to the Tualatin River, and on up the Tualatin as far as Forest Grove.

The canal was dug by hand by Chinese laborers and completed in 1871. (The locks were never built.) Use of the canal was limited because the water level was unreliable, and then in the 1880s the water transportation system was supplanted by a railroad system in the Tualatin Valley.

WALK

Walk up the dirt road to the green gauging station, where a trail begins between the road and the canal. The canal, only about 8 feet wide, resembles an overgrown stream. The banks are brushy but pretty when the leaves are out, and there is an aura of peace and isolation—a forgotten spot in the midst of a densely populated area. (Watch out for poison oak.)

The trail ends and development begins at a tennis court. From this point go back to the end of the road (which ends before the trail does) and take the left branch to make a loop trip back through fields to meet the road again at the gauging station. Follow the road back to the south across Childs Road and on down to the end at the Tualatin River. Here you can see the gate across the entrance of the canal which can be adjusted to regulate the level of Lake Oswego.

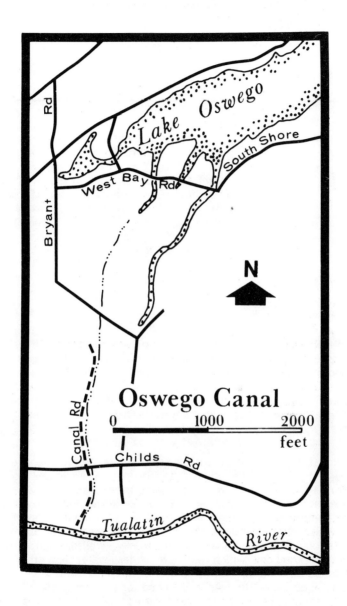

Lake Oswego

Rd

Bryant

West Bay Rd

South Shore

N

Oswego Canal

0   1000   2000
feet

Canal Rd

Childs Rd

Tualatin River

CAMASSIA NATURAL AREA AND WILDERNESS PARK

Walking Distance 1-2 miles or more

Time to Spend 1½ hours for each

Setting **Camassia.** Rocky and hilly with a dry microclimate
Wilderness Park. Typical second growth forest of Western Oregon; orchard

Distance from Downtown Portland 12 miles

Driving Directions S out of town on Macadam Ave. (Oregon 43) to West Linn. Turn R onto West "A" St.
Camassia. Park by the high school (the old building). From there walk W up Buse St. (It looks like someone's driveway.) A green sign reading "Foot Traffic Only" marks the entrance.
Wilderness Park. From West "A" St. turn R onto Skyline Drive just before the high school. Skyline curves around up the hill. Turn L into a parking lot beyond the signs.

Bus #36, Oregon City - S. Shore, goes along Oregon 43 through West Linn.

These two adjacent areas in West Linn are interesting to visit on the same day because they offer such a contrast. Wilderness Park is a good example of the kind of second-growth conifer forest usually found in the Portland area and represented in many of the walks in this book. In contrast, the Camassia Natural Area is a white-oak woodland much more typical of Southern Oregon or California.

CAMASSIA NATURAL AREA

Camassia is part of a bench on the bluffs 200 feet above the Willamette River. The unusual topography is attributed to the Missoula Flood, a catastrophic geologic event caused by warming climate at the end of the Ice Age. Evidence of the flood can be seen in scabbed areas, channels, and glacial erratics made of granite, a rock which otherwise does not occur in this area. The distinctive vegetation seems to be due to the rocky, well-drained surface scoured by the flood, which retains much less water than other soils around here.

The Camassia Natural Area is named for the camas plant, whose bulb was an important food source for the Indians. This is one of the few places you can see the beautiful blue-flowered camas today. Once common in the Willamette Valley, it is becoming scarce because of the spread of cities and cultivated fields. Here, too, wild roses are abundant, oak and madrone are common, and quaking aspen can be found. A number of rare plants have been spotted, and a plant list may be obtained from the Nature Conservancy.

Unfortunately two obnoxious plants are also well represented— Scotch broom has invaded widely, dominating the native vegetation, and poison oak grows so profusely along and over the trails that it is impossible to avoid except in winter.

This area is fascinating rather than beautiful. Perhaps because of its distinctiveness from the surrounding terrain, Camassia seems very remote and somewhat eerie even though you can always hear the traffic from I-205. The area is relatively open, and there are use trails all over. An old rock quarry provides rock walls for children and others who like to climb.

The uniqueness of the area was discovered by Murray Miller of Oregon City, and it was saved from development by the Nature Conservancy, which purchased it in the 1960s and leased it to Lewis & Clark College (This protected status was gained after the choicest part of the area had already been destroyed by the building of I-205).

WILDERNESS PARK

This is a good place for solitude in the woods. No one else was there on a sunny Sunday afternoon in spring.

Unfortunately the park lacks a rational system of trails. It is big enough in area for a long walk, but most of the neighborhood use trails and old road beds are relatively short dead ends. Hopefully someday a loop trail will be built on each side of the road. In the meantime we have made a rough attempt to indicate the locations of trails on the map.

A short loop walk is possible starting along the old road bed taking off from the south side of the parking lot. At a junction, take the trail to the right to circle back to the parking lot.

Wilderness Park can also be entered on foot from Sunset Park, a neighborhood playground on the west.

It is possible, though not easy, to descend from Wilderness Park into the adjoining Camassia area: enter Wilderness Park on the south side from Clark St., which bisects the park. Walk through the orchard where the trail forks. Keep right. Eventually the trail goes steeply down to the edge of Camassia. (The left branch crosses a stream and goes down the hill to the high school.)

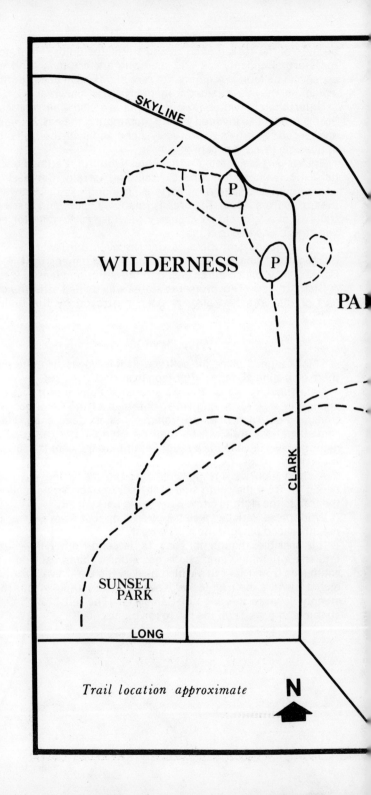

SKYLINE

WILDERNESS

P

P

PA

CLARK

SUNSET
PARK

LONG

Trail location approximate

N

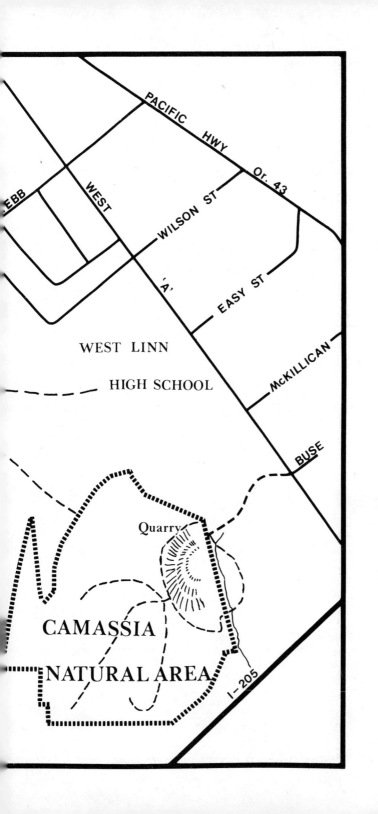

ELK ROCK ISLAND

Walking Distance	1 mile round trip
Time to Spend	About 2 hours. You may want to allow more time for swimming or picnicking.
Setting	Marsh, beach, woods
Distance from Downtown Portland	6¾ miles
Driving Directions	S on McLoughlin Blvd. (99E). Beyond downtown Milwaukie, turn off on River Rd. Turn R (W) toward the river at Sparrow. Go under the trestle to 19th. Park here. (These streets do not appear on Portland street maps, but have faith—they are there!)
Bus	#33, Oregon City/Superhighway, and #34, River Road, go along River Rd.

NOTE: Do not attempt this hike in times of flooding when access on foot may not be possible. If you object to getting your feet wet, it is best to skip this hike.

It is a thrill to discover this beautiful miniature island, with its beaches, rocks, and majestic woods, in the middle of our urban area. There is an amazing diversity of terrain. The north and west shores facing the Willamette have sandy crescent beaches. On the west shore there are also lots of moss-covered rocks to picnic and climb on. Inland is a tall, dense, second-growth mixed conifer forest in contrast to the willow brush and cottonwood found on other islands in the Willamette.

Few people hike to the island, but many boaters stop off to visit, and during the summer the Portland Park Bureau sponsors day-long children's excursions to the island. Unfortunately a good deal of garbage mars the scene.

WALK

To walk to the island, walk south from the junction of Sparrow and 19th to a blocked-off paved area. From there take the good trail west toward the river near the end of the paved area. (If you don't find this trail, you can still get to the island by wading through marsh grass.) The approach to the island is through tall grass and brush. Soon you emerge into a waste area of rock and scrub willow which may be covered with water but should be easy to wade.

A trail circles the island through the woods.

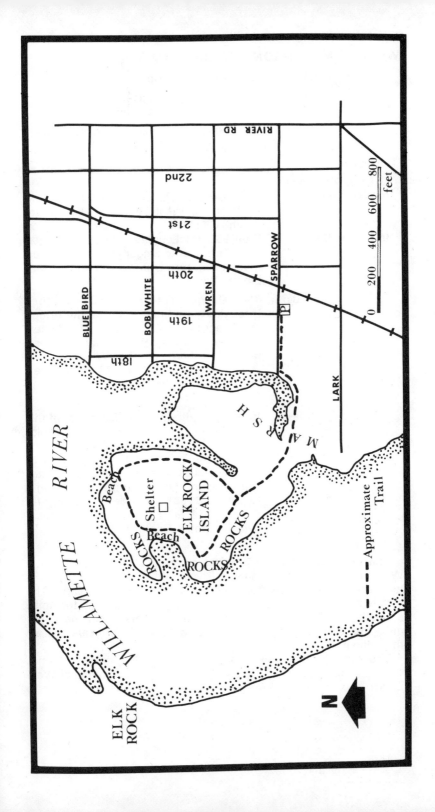

WEST LINN - OREGON CITY URBAN WALK

Walking Distance	3¼ miles round trip
Time to Spend	4 hours or more, depending on whether you tour the historic buildings
Setting	Sidewalks, scenic vistas and historic sites
Distance from Downtown Portland	13-14 miles
Driving Directions to West Linn	S on Oregon 43 (SW Macadam Ave. in Portland) to West Linn Inn. Park in lot behind City Hall.
to Oregon City	S on 99E (McLoughlin Blvd.) to Oregon City. Turn L onto Singer Hill Rd. to go up to top level, turn L on 7th St., and park at Library Park.
Bus	#36, Oregon City-South Shore, goes through West Linn and across the bridge into Oregon City. #33, Oregon City/Superhighway, and #34, River Road, go along the east shore of the Willamette to downtown Oregon City. #72, 82nd Ave., also passes through downtown Oregon City.
Eating Facilities	In keeping with the historical flavor of this urban walk, we recommend a choice between two historic spots at opposite ends of the tour: the West Linn Inn or Barclay House. (Call first to be sure they will be open.) Or, if you prefer to bring a lunch and eat outside, McLoughlin Promenade (#10 below) offers grass, benches, and sweeping views.

This urban walking tour provides a variety of interesting sights: Willamette Falls, the Willamette River from both shores, the locks in operation, and important historic sites in Oregon City. The negative aspects of the tour are that you are never far from the noise and exhaust of automobile traffic, and the fumes from the paper mills (the economic lifeblood of the two towns) permeate the air throughout the tour.

You can take this walk in either direction, beginning in either West Linn or Oregon City. We will describe it as beginning at West Linn.

1. Willamette Locks

An asphalt path starts to the left of the West Linn Inn. The path passes in front of the inn and then becomes an elevated wooden walkway along the side of the basalt cliff. Here you are walking between ivy-covered basalt on one side and big-leaf maple greenery on the other. There are occasional good views of the boats in the river and Oregon City on the other side. The walkway crosses the road and emerges into the open past the paper company parking lot and continues to the end of the path at the entrance to the locks.

This low flat area, for several centuries the site of an Indian fishing village, was subsequently the location of Linn City, the original town on the west shore of the river here. In the 1840s and '50s, Linn City was a thriving industrial town whose wharves, warehouses, and mills filled more than a mile of shoreline above and below the falls. This entire town was swept away in the flood of 1861 and never rebuilt.

A walkway is open to the public along the length of the four locks, which are used by a variety of river traffic, from small pleasure boats to barges carrying boxcars. The locks were built in 1870-72 by a private company to allow river traffic to bypass the falls, which had been a great barrier to travel in Indian and pioneer times. The locks were purchased by the U.S. government in 1915 and are now operated by the Army Corps of Engineers. They have issued a brochure (available at local Chambers of Commerce) providing more detailed information about the locks.

2. Oregon City-West Linn Bridge

To continue the walk, retrace your steps and walk across the bridge into Oregon City. The present bridge was opened in 1922 (replacing an earlier one constructed in 1888). To symbolize the joining of the two cities there was a large sentimental celebration, culminating in a wedding in the middle of the bridge of a girl from West Linn and a boy from Oregon City. The bridge was designed to be beautiful as well as utilitarian, and today it is the only bridge over the Willamette in the Portland area that seems to have retained a human scale. It is pleasant to walk across because it is a narrow bridge with only two lanes of traffic and wide sidewalks on either side. The bridge provides interesting views of the falls and the locks, which look much deeper from the front than from the side.

3. Walkway along East Bank of Willamette

Coming off the bridge in Oregon City, turn right (back toward the river) one block, cross the highway, and follow the walkway along the east side of the river for more views of the falls and the river. Here fishermen drop their lines a long way down off the cliff.

4. Municipal Elevator

When you have seen enough here, retrace your steps to 7th St. and proceed to the municipal elevator (easily visible!). Ascend the cliff either in the elevator or by means of the staircase next to it (#5 below).

By the 1870s Oregon City was a bustling city on two levels, and several sets of stairs had been built up the bluff. The first elevator was built in 1913 but not put into operation until 1915 because of debate over whether it should be powered by water or electricity. The Water Board thought that the diversion of water necessary to operate the elevator would reduce pressure in homes further up the hill. This turned out to be true, and water-users in those homes were always able to tell when the elevator was on its way up. The old elevator was finally connected to electricity in 1924. It was replaced by the present structure in 1954. Oregon City is probably the only town where commuters travel perpendicularly 90 feet between the business section on the lower level and their homes on the upper level.

At the top of the elevator there is a glass-enclosed observatory affording panaromic views including the I-205 bridge, the Oregon City-West Linn bridge, Publisher's Paper Co., and the river. In the foreground, you can see the Masonic Temple on Main St. between 7th and 8th St. (the building with the legend "Multnomah Lodge A.F. & A.M."). This is the oldest Masonic lodge west of the Missouri River, organized in 1846, with the charter brought across the plains by ox-team. There is also a good view of the County Courthouse at 8th and Main. The original plat of the city of San Francisco was filed here in 1850 when Oregon City had the only federal court and land office on the Pacific Coast.

5. Staircase

For fitness buffs here is an alternative to the elevator. The staircase is interesting because it parallels Singer Falls, now artifically channeled in cement troughs but nevertheless pleasant to see and hear on a hot day. Singer Falls was named for William Singer, who used it to power his flour mill in the 1880s. At the top of the staircase (and near the elevator) is a convenient pedestrian tunnel leading under busy Singer Hill Road to the McLoughlin House.

6. McLoughlin House, 7th and Center Streets (National Historic Monument

This house, which has been described as "colonial style, adapted to pioneer building conditions," was built in 1845 by Dr. John McLoughlin, after he resigned from a long, illustrious career as chief factor of the Hudson's Bay Company at Fort Vancouver. McLoughlin had been involved with Oregon City since 1828, when he started development in the area by establishing a sawmill at the falls.

A Park Service brochure succinctly states the importance of the house: "[It] represents the romantic epoch of Pacific Northwest history during the transition from the fur-trading era to that of settlement. It is a memorial to a man who generously aided the American settlers in establishing their homes in the Oregon Country."

The home originally stood on the waterfront where Publisher's Paper Mill is now. To escape destruction, it was moved to the present site in McLoughlin Park (land donated to the city by McLoughlin) in 1909.

The graves of Dr. McLoughlin and his wife have also been moved from past locations overtaken by progress to a site between McLoughlin House and the adjoining Barclay House.

McLoughlin House is open every day except Monday from 10 a.m. to 5 p.m. in summer and from 10 a.m. to 4 p.m. in winter. There is an admission charge.

7. Barclay House, 8th and Center Streets

This early home was built on the lower level of the town in 1846 and moved to the present site adjoining the McLoughlin House in 1937. Dr. Barclay had been chief surgeon at Fort Vancouver, where he became a close friend of Dr. McLoughlin. Dr. Barclay also practiced medicine in Oregon City and served as city councilman, coroner, school superintendent, and mayor. Currently the Barclay House (owned by the National Park Service) is operated as a tea room.

8. Historical Society Museum, 6th and Center Streets

The Clackamas County Historical Society maintains displays in the turn-of-the-century home of the pioneer Stevens-Crawford family. If you plan to go inside the museum, call in advance to see when it is open. There is a small admission charge.

The historical society is raising funds to build a new museum at 2nd and Tumwater Streets and may be located there by the time you read this. (This new location is still within easy walking distance for this tour.)

9. Library Park, 6th and Adams Sts.

Library Park is a large square shaded by beautiful old trees. The library is not particularly old, just a charming red and white brick building in early 20th century "library style." In front is an historical marker honoring the poet, Edwin Markham, born in Oregon City and renowned for his poem, "Man with a Hoe."

10. McLoughlin Promenade

The Promenade goes south from the elevator along the top of the bluff on land given to the city by McLoughlin and nicely landscaped in recent years. The promenade offers sweeping views but is dominated most of the way by the sight, sound, and smell of the paper company. Toward the end, the promenade descends gradually from the top of the bluff, crosses 99E on a pedestrian overpass, and continues to the Falls Vista Viewpoint on 99E.

11. Falls Vista

This is the spot for the closest, most spectacular view of Willamette Falls. The water here is spilling 41 feet over a horseshoe-shaped basaltic ledge, and the crest of the falls is more than 3000 feet long.

The falls was an even more awesome sight in pioneer times before most of the water was syphoned off in flumes for operating the mills. Industrial use of the falls began in 1828 when Dr. John McLoughlin (see #6 above) established a sawmill. A woolen mill was established in 1864, the first paper mill came in 1867, and in 1889 electricity was produced for transmission to Portland. (This was the first long-distance commercial electric power transmission in the United States.)

CANEMAH CEMETERY

Walking Distance	1 mile round trip
Time to Spend	1 hour
Setting	Peaceful overgrown cemetery in the woods
Distance from Downtown Portland	9 miles
Driving Directions	S on McLoughlin Blvd. (99E) through Oregon City. Turn L onto Hedges, L on Third, R on Ganong leading to 4th; L on Blanchard leading to 5th. Park where you see a cable across a dirt road (Cemetery Rd.)
Bus	#72, 82nd Ave., and #33, Oregon City/ Superhighway, go along 99E.

Follow the dirt road through fir woods to Canemah Cemetery, a pioneer burying ground with markers dating from the 1850s. This location on a bluff high above the river is especially appropriate for some of those buried here: headstones tell us of one person "drowned in the Willamette River" and three others "lost over the Willamette Falls." The tranquillity may soon be shattered, as a wide swath of the woods southwest of the cemetery has recently been cleared.

Canemah Cemetery is located above the early town site of Canemah. Because of its location at the head of Willamette Falls, the terminus of upper river traffic on the Willamette, a thriving shipping town grew up here. The port flourished until the decline of river traffic in the 1880s. Before the settlers came, this portage point had been an important Indian campsite called Canemah, "the canoe place."

ENVIRONMENTAL LEARNING CENTER, CLACKAMAS COMMUNITY COLLEGE

Walking Distance	1 mile
Time to Spend	1 hour
Setting	Miniature wildlife refuge
Distance from Downtown Portland	12½ miles
Driving Directions	S on 99E (McLoughlin Blvd.) to Oregon City. Go up the hill and out of town on 213 to Clackamas Community College. Take the left branch on the Campus Loop Rd. past most of the buildings and playing fields.
Bus	#33, Oregon City/Superhighway

Though more than a mile of trails circles through the area, the Environmental Learning Center provides an ambience to experience rather than a place for strenuous walking.

Here is a remarkable example of the renewal of a natural area despoiled by industrial waste. A diverse ecological world has been created on this small site (3½ acres), formerly a settling pond for cannery wastes. (The cannery building, now an art center, still stands north of the Learning Center.)

Dense plantings of native and common garden plants plus an abundance of water in the ponds have created a haven for wildlife. More than 70 species of birds have been observed; and when we visited, tame rabbits and muskrats followed us around! More than 250 species of plants can be seen here, many identified by labels.

The Environmental Learning Center was created by community effort. Volunteers built the trails, bridges, and dams, and contributed the plants from their own gardens. Boy Scouts built and installed 40 nesting boxes. The area is maintained by college students, CETA personnel, and Community Corrections workers.

The staff of the center is planning an ambitious program of environmental education. A station instructional system consisting of self-instructing tapes to be located at 19 points throughout the site is being prepared, an information center building has been designed, and workshops on appropriate technology are projected.

While you are on campus, you may want to take the opportunity to see the flower gardens and the start of an arboretum (see map).

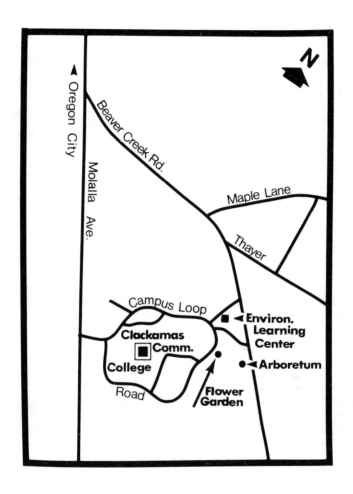

McIVER STATE PARK

Walking Distance	3-5 miles
Time to Spend	½ day or more
Setting	Vast open fields with wide vistas; open or dense woods along the shore
Distance from Downtown Portland	25 miles
Driving Directions	S from Portland on 99E (McLoughlin Blvd.) Take exit for Highway 224 and continue on it to Carver. Turn R across the bridge, then L onto Springwater Road. The park entrance is 9 miles from Carver.
Bus	No service

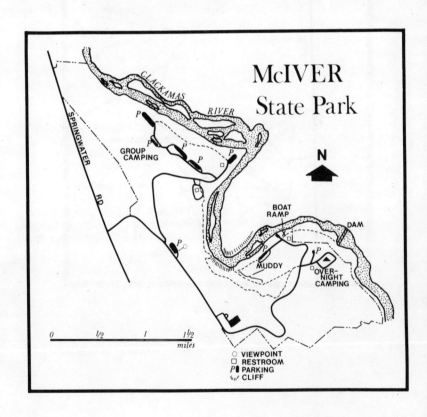

This large, handsome park (847 acres) is situated on a series of terraces above the Clackamas River near Estacada. The Clackamas is a swift young river with many exciting rapids which attract whitewater rafters. (Inexperienced people should beware, however, since some drown every year.) The river also has a good reputation for fishing. Perhaps the most enthusiastic fisherman in these waters was the famous English writer, Rudyard Kipling, who spent 37 minutes landing a 12-pound fighting salmon with a 8-ounce rod, and then wrote:

"I have lived! The American continent may now sink under the sea, for I have taken the best that it yields."

Though another popular activity here is large group picnics, the park is so vast that it should still be possible to find relative solitude.

In the east section of the park, along the trail from the parking lot to the shore, there is an area of mature yew trees worth noticing. It is interesting to see these trees growing tall, straight, and full, in contrast to the small scraggly form which yew usually takes in the Northwest woods.

WALKS

Where the entrance road forks, you can take either branch to get to the more than 3 miles of hiking trails indicated on the map. These trails wind through lush second-growth forest which is home to many animals, including deer.

In the east section of the park note that the trail up from the shore to the overnight camp area is apt to be extremely muddy—best left for a dry spell in summer or fall, or a cold snap in winter when the mud is frozen.

There is other good walking territory besides the hiking trails. For a view of River Mill Dam, you can walk upstream about half a mile from the boat ramp at the east end of the park. Or, in the northwest section of the park, you can roam across broad rolling lawns accented by large spruce and Douglas fir trees—an area where the previous owner had started to develop a golf course.

MOUTH OF THE CLACKAMAS RIVER

Walking Distance	2 miles round trip
Time to Spend	1½ hours, longer if fishing or swimming
Setting	Stony shoreline, old roadbed, open or brushy
Distance from Downtown Portland	11 miles
Driving Directions	S on 99E (McLoughlin Blvd.) to Gladstone. Turn off on the *last* road to the R before the bridge over the Clackamas River. (This road turns off beyond the light and between the Texaco station and Webster Ford.
Bus	#33, Oregon City/Superhighway, #34, River Road, and #72, 82nd Ave.

This point, where the Clackamas River flows into the Willamette, is a major open space in the midst of the metropolitan area. It is not really a pretty place and is too disturbed and noisy to be called a natural area, but it does offer a mile of river access and vistas of two major rivers.

(Clackamette Park is located on the south shore of the Clackamas here. The entrance is to the right off McLoughlin just after you cross the bridge. Since this park is almost always crowded and noisy with many power boats launching and landing, we prefer the north shore of the Clackamas.)

WALK

From the parking area on the north side of the Clackamas River, you can follow the shore of the Willamette north for a short distance. When we were there fishermen were doing well. For a longer walk, go south along the Willamette, then turn east, and continue upstream along the Clackamas. You can walk along either the stony shore or an old roadbed. This route takes you past a duck pond, under 99E, and upstream approximately as far as the railroad bridge. (You may not get quite that far in times of high water.) It is interesting to watch rafters here going through the last major rapids on the Clackamas. Occasionally the river is warm enough for swimming.

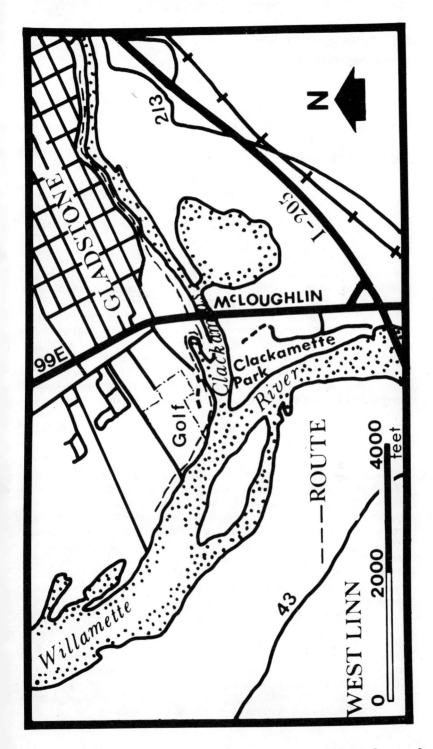

CHAMPOEG STATE PARK

Walking Distance	½ - 8 miles
Time to Spend	½ day for walking ½ day for visiting the museums
Setting	Wooded shore with occasional access to the water; fields
Distance from Downtown Portland	28 miles
Driving Directions	S on I-5 to the Aurora/Donald exit (better than the Champoeg exit). Turn right, drive about 6 miles, and then follow signs to Champoeg.
Bus	No bus service

Champoeg State Park has many attractions. It is ideal for picnicking, with shaded tables, open fields, and river access. Overnight camping is also available, and in summer the parks branch provides a naturalist program, including guided walks, activities for children, and evening programs. The new Visitor Center and two historical museums are worth a visit. Besides all this, of course, Champoeg offers several good areas for walking. (This is a heavily used park, so for privacy, avoid the Riverside Picnic Area and the bike trail on Sunday afternoons.)

The park has quite a variety of interesting vegetation—oak groves, locust groves, many ash trees, as well as a variety of ornamentals. There is a small arboretum of native trees and shrubs, many of them labeled, near the Riverside Picnic Area.

HISTORY

Though Champoeg is a pastoral area today, it was an important habitation in the past. This natural meadow was once the location of a large Indian village, "Champooick." The name is a combination of French and Indian words meaning "field of roots," referring to the camas roots which used to grow here and were an important source of food for the Indians. The first white settlement was a Hudson's Bay Post established in 1831. Champoeg is most important in Oregon history as the location of the meeting at which the Oregon government was founded in 1843 even though the Provisional Government headquarters was moved to Oregon City in 1844, the town continued to grow through the 1840s and '50s, until it was literally washed away by a record flood in 1861.

A wealth of historical information is available for those who are interested. The State Parks Department has provided an impressive new Visitor Center containing modern interpretive exhibits about the history of the Willamette Valley and Champoeg. The D.A.R. maintains two museums full of interesting items from the 1850s: The Robert Newell Residence represents the home of one of the political leaders at Champoeg, while the Pioneer Mother's Home exemplifies the simple log cabins of earlier settlers. Two good books with information on Champoeg are *Champoeg: Place of Transition* by J.A. Hussey, and *Willamette Landings* by Howard McKinley Corning.

WALKS

Riverside Picnic Area

A short loop trail goes near the river here (see map). You can also explore the arboretum area near the pavilion.

River trail

From the Pioneer Mother's Home to the Oak Grove Picnic Area. This walk also starts at the beginning of the bike trail. Start walking along the barred gravel road through the group camp area. This eventually becomes a path passing through a sheep meadow and woods near the river.

Bike trail to Butteville

3½ miles one way. Look for the sign "Begin Bike Trail" near the Pioneer Mother's Home. This mostly flat, asphalt trail passes through open fields and wooded areas near the water. You will know you have arrived at Butteville when you see the attractive facade of the Butteville General Store.

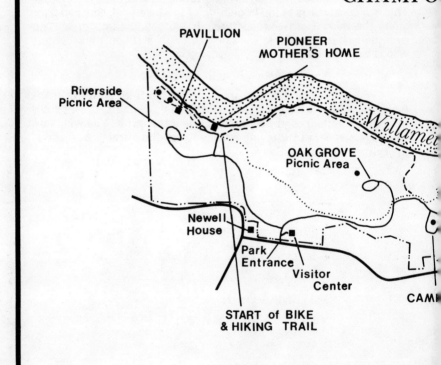

CHAMPO

PAVILLION

PIONEER
MOTHER'S HOME

Riverside
Picnic Area

Willame

OAK GROVE
Picnic Area

Newell
House

Park
Entrance

Visitor
Center

CAM

START of BIKE
& HIKING TRAIL

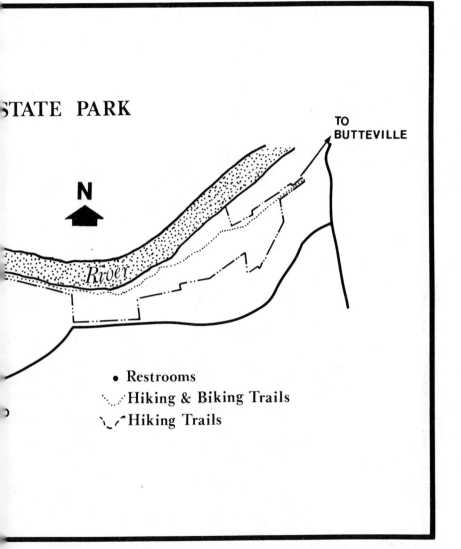

STATE PARK

TO
BUTTEVILLE

N

River

- Restrooms
- Hiking & Biking Trails
- Hiking Trails

INDEX TO WALKS